The Little Book
of Spirit
Readings

The Ghostly Bits

T0050526

First published by O Books, 2008
O Books is an imprint of John Hunt Publishing Ltd., The Bothy, Deershot Lodge, Park Lane, Ropley,
Hants, SO24 0BE, UK
office1@o-books.net
www.o-books.net

Distribution in:

UK and Europe
Orca Book Services
orders@orcabookservices.co.uk
Tel: 01202 665432 Fax: 01202 666219
Int. code (44)

USA and Canada
NBN
custserv@nbnbooks.com
Tel: 1 800 462 6420 Fax: 1 800 338 4550

Australia and New Zealand
Brumby Books
sales@brumbybooks.com.au
Tel: 61 3 9761 5535 Fax: 61 3 9761 7095

Far East (offices in Singapore, Thailand,
Hong Kong, Taiwan)
Pansing Distribution Pte Ltd
kemal@pansing.com
Tel: 65 6319 9939 Fax: 65 6462 5761

South Africa
Alternative Books
altbook@peterhyde.co.za
Tel: 021 555 4027 Fax: 021 447 1430

Text copyright Collette Star 2008

Design: Stuart Davies

ISBN: 978 1 84694 158 0

A CIP catalogue record for this book is available
from the British Library.

Printed by Digital Book Print

O Books operates a distinctive and ethical publishing philosophy in
all areas of its business, from its global network of authors to
production and worldwide distribution.
This book is produced on FSC certified stock, within ISO14001
standards. The printer plants sufficient trees each year through
the Woodland Trust to absorb the level of emitted carbon in
its production.

The Little Book of Spirit Readings

The Ghostly Bits

Collette Star

BOOKS

Winchester, UK
Washington, USA

CONTENTS

Foreword	*viii*
Brentford; *Tap Dancing*	1
Malden Street Fair; *Apple Pie*	2
Somerset; *Two Husbands*	4
Kingston; *God, Does My Bum Look Big in this?*	5
Cambridge; *Three in a Bed*	6
Strawberry Hill; *Man Who Couldn't Get It Up*	7
Regent's Park; *Butlins....*	8
Basingstoke; *My Only Black Suit*	9
Somerset; *Oranges & Lemons*	10
Somerset; *Recorder Girl*	11
Surbiton; *Man at Surbiton*	12
Basingstoke; *Cut Ginger*	14
Dolphin Nursery; *Still Birth*	15
Kew; *Pub at Kew*	16
Oxford; *12 Men & True*	18
Oxford; *The Girl with Two Shadows*	19
Oxford; *Is she any good?*	20
Oxford; *The end is not nigh*	20
Camden Town; *'Should she or shouldn't she?'*	22
Camden Lock; *From Gunslinger to Pussycat*	23
Strawberry Hill; *Over the Strawberry Hill or just a small problem?*	25
Somerset; *The Little Girl*	26
Somerset; *Pretty **Wo**-Man*	27
Strawberry Hill; *The bridge away from troubled waters*	28
Somerset; *No title*	29
Somerset; *'Tell 'im to eff-off'!'*	30
Bristol; *Chinese Customs*	31
Bristol; *Death Becomes Her*	31
Wales; *Breakfast at Tiffany's*	32
Camden; *Manic Depressive*	33

Camden; *Drugs 'R' us*   34

Camden; *The Witch Doctor*   35

Camden; *The Aussie floor-layer; he'd lay anything…*   36

Camden; *Wants Her Cake and Eat It....*   37

Camden; *The blind leading the blind....*   38

Camden; *It's a Posh Chinese, well dressed Affair*   39

Kingston; *A 400 year old Gypsy........ and still looking fit*   40

Camden; *Japanese bowing*   41

Camden; *A woman I could not do....*   42

Epson Races; *Where's one when you want one?*   42

Epson Races; *You are going along way-away to a far off land....*   44

Epson Races; *The bruised skating Healer...*   45

Bristol; *Steve's £80,000 'accounting error'.....*   46

Dunfermline; *A little help from a friend...*   47

Greenford; *Uncomfortable with her Step-Dad......*   48

Greenford; *Vanity......*   48

Ealing; *There are many paths to my father's house; but all lead there.*   50

Esher Fair; *'I'm not being rude, but do **Shut up!**'*   51

Esher Fair; *Washing Line........*   52

Esher; *Stu-pot Stuart....*   53

Clapham; *He's as cold as ice............Oh, but what a lovely man....*   55

Cambridge; *Talking to walls? Each to their own, I suppose.........*   56

Cambridge; *Eyes wide and a shocked expression...*   57

Esher Fair; *A Medium pipe dream.....*   58

Somerset; *Mother knows best.......*   59

Somerset; *For he has all of the answers....*   60

Ealing; *Three in a bed, and the Granny said.....*   60

Ealing; *Run rabbit, run rabbit, run, run, run...*   61

Ealing; *The melting Ice Maiden...*   62

Ealing; *Teachers always want the last word......*   63

Ealing; *A caring person and their money are unfortunately parted easily.......*   64

Earl's Court; *Jumping Jack Flash....*   65

Camden; *Language problems? Not a problem, when you're dead.*   66

Regent's Park; *An unexpected lesson...in her thirst for knowledge...*   67

Regent's Park; *A little ray of light in the darkness....*   68

Regent's Park; *The Spirit Fairy, a fluffy dog and Alexandria.....*   69

Somerset; *The Potato men....*   72

Somerset; *Being undemanding, is it hereditary?*   74

Bristol; *The Black Car will come for him soon.*   74

Bristol; *No escape from 'The Boys in Blue'*   75

Bristol; *She's a bit of an old Croc...*   76

Cambridge; *A stony past...*   77

Cambridge; *Sisters are doing for themselves.....*   78

Greenford; *Just keeps talking.....*   79

Kent; *A butcher, a Baker and a French Waiter?*   80

Camden; *Brian? That's a funny name for an Angel.*   81

Watford; *Her Blood Red Dress.*   83

Scotland, Isle of Bute 3rd floor; *The mystery tinkler...*   85

Scotland, Isle of Bute, 2nd floor; *We met upon the stairs.*   85

Scotland, Edinburgh; *The Haunted B&B.........*   86

Epson; *I didn't go under the Mistletoe....*   87

Ealing; *Carry your guilt, no more.*   88

Ealing; *'Give them my love'*   89

Scotland; *An Invitation, Oooo I like a bit of fun!*   92

Ealing; *Sucking lemons*   94

Kew Fayre; *'I will walk the walk with you, till the end of the walk'*   95

Kew Fayre; *Fudge for Africa*   97

Kingston; *A confessional with no judgement*   98

S.A.G.B HQ, Belgrave square; *Spirit are wonderful*   100

Teddington Lock; *A mother never really forgets....*   103

Somerset; *Never say goodbye.*   104

Elephant & Castle; *Mixing Spirits*   105

Greenford; *Green Condom*   107

Thames Riverside; *You've gotta have faith...*   108

Kew Fayre; *The Wonderful Love*   110

Putney; *Do you mind!........ Ma'am....*   110

Brockwell Park; *I don't look when they have sex!*   112

Somerset; *Oh Susan; your Mum knows now......*   113

Basingstoke; *Sunshine Face*   116

Cambridge; *A Clean Habit.*   118

Cambridge; *Resistance Healing*   120

London; *Love thy Neighbour......*   121

London; *Anthony, my dad and my uncle.*   124

Acknowledgements   128

Collette Star

Collette Star is so many things: mother, grandmother, friend, confidante, healer, actress, singer, story-teller. She is also a clairvoyant medium, blessed with an extraordinary gift. She is able to help people in this life by communicating with those in the next.

Born in Dublin just after the end of the Second World War, Collette spent her first few years in hospital, suffering from acute TB. At times she was so ill that she very nearly died, but with characteristic determination and indomitable spirit she fought her way back to health so that she could re-join her family, who had since moved to London.

But in a rundown council flat in smoggy Lambeth, it was soon apparent that Collette wasn't like other children, for this little girl saw ghosts. Her parents, who were strict Catholics, were mortified, and they punished her severely, convinced it had to be the work of the Devil. Poor Collette became so terrified that she prayed for the visions to stop, and thankfully they did, so that she could get on and grow up like any other child on the street.

Collette was more athletic than academic, and she excelled at sports and on the stage. She was a champion swimmer and won countless dancing competitions; by the age of 14 she sang solo at the Royal Albert Hall for the Lord Mayor of Lambeth to riotous applause. Her bubbly personality and pretty good looks ensured she had many suitors, and soon after school she married her first husband.

Unfortunately, he didn't like Collette performing in clubs and pubs, and he moved her away from her hectic and happy social life in Battersea to sleepy Sutton, where she was soon busy bringing up two young children. Away from her family for the first time, the stricture against the otherworldly visions weakened, and she became aware of a ghost in her house. But he was not a nice presence, and he began to torment her.

Driven to distraction, Collette eventually moved out, only to discover her husband had been seeing another woman all the while they had been married. Quickly divorced, Collette was drawn to a spiritualist church, where she would meet new types of people, including her second husband, an altogether different man from the first. He immediately sensed her psychic abilities, and introduced her to people who were not frightened by but understood her gift. There then followed a time of great healing and learning, and Collette had two more children in much happier circumstances.

But it all came to an abrupt halt when her husband suddenly died. Collette was now on her own with four children to support, and all the good of the past few years seemed to be coming undone, when Spirit intervened, and she was offered a house in Stevenage. Collette took her children away from the pain in London and settled into a new life in Hertfordshire, for the first time accepting and developing her gift as a healer. She cured many people, and found many more coming to her for help, which she was able to give by reading Tarot cards with great success.

Feeling much better in herself, Collette joined a local theatre troupe and got back to performing on the stage. This proved to be a truly happy and peaceful time for her, marred only by the death of her father, when a new man appeared on the scene, who would become husband number three. Blinded by love and not trusting her inner doubts, she allowed this man to persuade her to leave her abundant life to move to Scotland to run a chicken farm.

By now her eldest children had left home, so Collette sold her house and made the move North with her two youngest children. She worked her fingers to the bone in an attempt to make a go of the enterprise, only to find out that her husband was a conman, and that he had fleeced her of everything and saddled her with huge debts.

She moved back to London with her children, penniless and homeless. Forced to live in a rough part of South London, after the fourth burglary, she borrowed a van and drove her sons to Devon to try to begin life anew. Over time, she found a place to live, and her two remaining boys grew up and left home. But cut off from her family and friends, and no longer reading cards or working as a healer, Collette sank into a deep depression, which was exacerbated by the death of her mother.

She had become suicidal when Spirit again intervened, and her Dad appeared to her as a ghost. This time he was not the angry father punishing her for seeing visions, but an understanding man who had come to reveal her true destiny to her as a clairvoyant medium.

Soon after, Collette's sons moved back home, and she was guided by Spirit to return to Battersea in South London, where she had grown up and always felt at home. For the first time, she was able to commit fully to her calling, and she began to give spirit readings to people seeking help.

Collette was then guided by Spirit to draw her own pack of Tarot Cards, based on flowers. These beautiful cards reflect something of her personality: they are vibrant and full of life, but also gentle and soothing. It was at this point that Collette was finally able to see that the trials and tribulations she had endured for so many years had been one long preparation for her unique calling to reveal messages from the spirit world to the bereaved. Life had taught her the importance of being compassionate and non-judgemental, and also how to take the edge off suffering with humour, love and good cheer. She had also learned how to communicate easily and effectively with people from all walks of life.

Significantly, throughout her long journey, Collette never lost her fun-loving nature and profound love of life, nor the gentleness which is characteristic of a true spiritual healer. Guided by Spirit, she has since written children's stories and devised healing meditations. She has helped many thousands of people, easing their pain and strengthening their connection to loved ones now departed.

In this extraordinary book, she has recorded some of the most remarkable and memorable of her spirit readings. As you read them, not only will you be entertained, but you will also find yourself gently healed.

Anthony James Taylor

Brentford;

Tap Dancing

A tall, nice-looking educated black girl sat down before me. As she did so, the face of a man appeared, then a whole body. I thought, 'I'll wait a minute to see if he's going to stay.' And he did.

As I laid down her cards, I described to her what this man looked like, with his chiselled face and his bony wiry body. Once I'd said this to her, he amazed me by performing a sort of tap dance, expressing his excitement that he had got through and that he could communicate with me, and that what he was saying was being relayed exactly to her.

'He says that he is your grandfather, and that you never knew him, but that you knew of him.' With that he did another dance of excitement. He showed me a cigarette and a bottle of beer, and when I told her what he was showing me another tap dance followed. I described his grey suit and hat, so again – you've guessed it – another tap dance, but now with the addition of clapping, he was so excited that I'd got it right!

'He says that he came from Trinidad (well I don't know one foreign country from another!) He also says that he left your grand-mother to make his millions in England in the 50's. She was a big woman and he is showing me her 'big-end'!

What did surprise me was that he could show me a woman's 'big bottom' that was sitting on a chair: and of a lady who is still alive on this earth – as I later found out! It just goes to show you that thoughts become things in Spirit.

'He never came back to Trinidad, he just womanised, smoked and drunk a lot. He basically wasted his life – not like you,' I told her. I also informed her that he said every time I told her things he would dance and clap. This was a very funny reading!

When we finished she told me that there was a picture of her granddad on the mantelpiece looking just as I described, and that he never did come back. I was right, she never knew him, but she did know of him. And yes, it was Trinidad, and her Grandmother was very big back then, but she wasn't so big now.

I said to the young lady, 'Don't say anything about me, just get the picture and let your grandmother talk about him.

Then when she has finished, play this tape to her. Tell her he says he is sorry, please forgive him, but he is here to help her now.

* * *

Malden Street Fair;
Apple Pie

An older lady sat down and suddenly an apple pie flew past our heads. It just kept encircling us both, around and around it went. It wasn't a real apple pie, and the lady couldn't see it.

Spirit only took it away when I told the lady about what I could see.

She looked at me as if I were... well, not quite all there. I did apologise for it, but I also had to explain that I can't get rid of whatever I am seeing or feeling until I tell the other person about it; but that's just the way my guides work with me.

I brushed it off by saying, 'Let's just carry on with the cards.'

Then suddenly I was a small child in a big country kitchen, my nose was just touching the top of the large wooden table, and there was an older lady rolling out some pastry. I described to the lady sitting opposite what I was seeing and what the surroundings were. And asked if she knew of such a place or experience, she replied with a resounding, 'No!'

She followed up from the resounding 'No!' by saying that she knew nothing of the apple pie, nor of the table, or anything of what I was saying. With that the spirit lady came rushing back and said that she lived in the middle of nowhere. I relayed this but again the lady said 'No!' I was then shown by the spirit lady a big garden full of apple trees, whose fruit was used in the apple pies. I presented this to her, and you've guessed it; the lady still, said 'No!'

I continued with her consultation.

I then said to the lady that 'The spirit lady that is with us tells me that her husband was away a lot, and that he worked on the railway. And you would visit her as a child, because she was lonely.'

Again, and now tryingly, she replied with the usual 'No!'

I then asked the spirit lady to find something else; something of such firm evidence that it could not be rebuked.

I was shown a red brick house. On conveying this information to the lady she said, 'NO!'

I said to the lady, 'I am stuck in this kitchen and I can't get out of the door, why? Why?' Then suddenly I was made aware of a lot of geese passing the kitchen door, which as a child this lady had been terrified of. This I quickly imparted to the lady, and just then her face said it all! She gasped,

'That's my auntie, and she's been... dead for years!'

'Well,' I said, 'she's here!'

Her face was a picture when she was recalling the memories – it was so alive it glowed with delight. She was brimming with excitement. 'Yes, yes,' she babbled incessantly, 'I used to stay with my auntie when I was a little girl, and yes, yes, my uncle was always working and she made lots of pies and yes, yes, it was a red brick house in the countryside, it was isolated with nobody about, and the geese, yes, the geese, I hated them so much! I would stand at the kitchen door terrified to go out.'

After she had calmed down from her elation she apologised for not understanding the first time, or the second........ Or the third.

We both laughed because she couldn't understand to start with, but I was so quietly grateful for the hard work that spirit had to do, and for giving me the courage to continue and not to be disheartened or to give up where many others may have.

We continued with the rest of her cards, after which both she and her auntie left together.

* * *

Somerset;
Two Husbands

A woman sat down, she was quite a tall woman. I thought she looked familiar.

As I was shuffling the cards a tall man appeared beside her. He just blurted out 'I like the bathroom' I told her this, and she just smiled *(as not to give the game away)*. He then took me into her kitchen and showed me the dark wooden units, saying I like the kitchen, its nice' I told her what he was doing and saying.

'Yes,' she said, 'I have just moved house.'

I said, 'Well, he likes it there.' I stopped to ponder before adding, 'I am very confused… because this is your husband who is dead. But I feel that you are married to one who is alive.'

She got excited and said, 'Yes, yes, yes, that's right!!'

With that I laughed. I said, 'You live with two husbands because he is always there! He says that 'he will look after you, the same as you looked after him. He tells me that you washed him, fed him and bed-bathed him, and other personal care too. And that it was very difficult for you both' He is now crying and I am upset too, and you. That's all three of us then… He sends so much love to

4

you… You both look like each other – that's weird!' I remarked and she agreed.

I then started to do her cards for her future.

She said to me, 'You do know me; I came to you last year.'

'I'm sorry' I said 'but I do see a lot of people'

'I'm back because you are the only medium who can get my husband for me. I've tried for years' said the lady as she smiled.

'Well it's probably that we are compatible,' I said, 'and not that I am wonderful or that other mediums are no good. I think you have to be compatible with the sitter, and most important of all with the spirit that wishes to communicate.

That is *my* opinion though… See you next year, and God bless!'

* * *

Kingston;
God, Does My Bum Look Big in this?

A young girl of only about seventeen years sat down. As I was shuffling the cards I could see a clothes rack with a lot of clothes hanging on it, and I was browsing through them.

I leant towards the girl and tried to explain what I was seeing,

'I seem to be in a shop, and taking some items into the fitting room, trying them on, and asking Spirit, 'Do I look good in this, or not? Does my Bum look big in this?'

She let out a surprised laugh and said 'yes, I do that all the time'

Well, I thought it was hilarious! I had never heard of this before.

After reading her future we said goodbye.

'And thank you for the laugh!' I said finally.

She was a nice girl.

* * *

Cambridge;

Three in a Bed

In from the pouring rain came a young woman of about twenty-six. She sat down with some real stinking attitude! Folding her arms she demanded:

'Well, are you any good then?'

I looking over my half-rimmed glasses I calmly replied 'Some people think so and always come back. It's not for me to say and I cannot be my judge'

'Well,' she said aggressively, 'what are your qualifications?'

I thought, 'God, I've a right one here!'

'Well,' I said, 'Spirit didn't send me any certificates. But then, Jesus never walked around with any either. And personally I think that he did a good job. All I can say, is if you're not happy with your reading you can have a full refund. Our reason to be here is not to rip people off; it's to connect them to spirit, so that they know for sure that they are not alone.'

The girl now seemed to relax a bit. When she started to shuffle the cards I suddenly felt very upset and all alone in this world, and I asked the girl whether this was how she felt.

She started to cry.

I said, 'You are not alone because your spirit guides and guardian angels are telling me how you feel. The man in your life, or somebody that you are close to, has stabbed you in the back after you gave them what they wanted, and they have done the dirty on you as repayment.'

'Yes,' she said through her sobbing.

I said to her, 'there seems to be three people in the same bed, two women and one man.'

'Yes, yes, I am so ashamed of it all! She was my friend and it all went wrong. He wanted this and I said okay. She got pregnant, because behind my back he was seeing her. They now live together and she is four months gone; and I am alone...' she said, sobbing continuously throughout.

'I am not here to judge,' I said to her.

'But to my mind this situation was a recipe for somebody – if not everybody – to be hurt one way or another.

'Please be nice to yourself in the future – and respect yourself,' I continued.

Her future reading with the cards turned out not too bad – much better than had happened so far.

When we parted company she took away two complimentary meditation CDs. It's something that I often do when a person is in need and that I feel that they cannot afford them. She left much happier and unburdened.

But before she left I asked her if I needed any certificates. She smiled and said, 'No, I am so sorry. You should be highly recommended.'

I said, 'Yes, I am, that's why your guide sent you to me. You can't get any higher recommendation than that, they know what they're doing. Unfortunately, we humans don't always do what is best.

'Goodbye. I'll see you next year, and may your God look after you.'

* * *

Strawberry Hill;
Man Who Couldn't Get It Up

A young black man sat down. He was very nervous.

As his consultation started a picture remained continuously in my head and I just couldn't shake it off. The picture was of a very limp penis.

All throughout his future reading I thought I was going mad; there it was this limp thing. How on God's earth was I going to approach this?

The only way I can, and do – 'straight from the shoulder'

He was quite happy with his reading, but still very quiet until I said,'Spirit keeps showing me a limp penis, and they keep telling me that you are very worried about it.'

Well, his eyes nearly popped out of his head!

I said, 'It's okay, it's all part of life. The problem is, you're getting caught up in a spiral, it's like a vicious circle, and the more you're worrying, the worse it will become. Possibly the best thing for you to do is to see your doctor and get some Viagra. Just half should do. This will get you out of the mind-set and out of the spiral. Next time I see you your confidence will have returned and you won't need the pills.'

He shook my hand, and with a big smiling face he said,

'I'll see you next year!'

When he left, I was so pleased I'd had the courage to say what spirit had shown me, because that's all he wanted a reading for, to try and understand what was going on.

I have to laugh at the difficult situations and things that spirit gets me to do. I think it's simply that they know I won't get in their way and that I will do their bidding, without altering things or being afraid too much.

* * *

Regent's Park;
Butlins....

A middle-aged man sat down. 'How do you work?' he asked me as I was shuffling the cards.

I explained that I would tell him how his life was right now and a little of the past, in order to give credibility to what I would say for his three-month future. He seemed pleased with this.

'Why do I keep seeing this chest of drawers?' I said.

'I don't know,' he quickly replied.

I then said 'It won't go away; and I've seen it four times now!'
He looked at me a bit oddly.

We carried on, but as the reading progressed the chest of drawers appeared again, so I described it.

'It's cheap – sorry – but it is a cheap chest. And in the second drawer there is a picture of a family at Butlins holiday camp... You were all having a good time...'

'Yes,' he said, 'that's where mum kept the picture of us all at Butlins, in the second drawer.'

'well she is not showing me herself at this moment, but this is her way of making herself known to you, her way of saying: "Son, I am still with you."

He was very pleased to have got such a good piece of evidence. I then progressed on to his future.

* * *

Basingstoke;
My Only Black Suit

The nice lady sat down, a bit on the fidgety side due to her being a little nervous.

Just then a man dressed all in black appeared by her side. He was tall and thin with sunken eyes and hollow cheeks; he also had a greyish-yellowish complexion. He showed me the coffin that he was put into, as well as his black suit. Still retaining his sense of humour, he laughed whilst holding out his arms and shrugging his wiry shoulders and said 'Well! My only Black Suit!'

He showed the make-up that was put on him, including the blusher and lipstick. I asked him 'what he was here to say' At this point the lady was completely unaware of anything that was going on.

He asked me to say thank you to his daughter, and all of the family, for not looking at him before or during the funeral. I relayed this to the lady, and then her eyes welled up with tears, which overflowed and ran down her face. At the same time she put

her hand to her mouth and gasped in disbelief.

'Yes, yes!' she said. 'He was riddled with cancer, and he looked so bad the undertakers advised us not to look; so we didn't.'

'Well, I said, he's fine now, and he thanks you for keeping the memory of him as he was before.'

So we got started on the reading for her future. When we parted she left happier and a lot less nervous.

* * *

Somerset;
Oranges & Lemons

A young dark-faced girl sat down. She was only about 20 years of age.

As I started to shuffle the cards I could hear a woman singing:

'*Aye, Aye, Aye, Aye, like you very much!*'

I had to sing it out loud to her and explain that it was an old hit song by Carman Miranda that this woman just kept on singing. But the young girl had no knowledge of this, so I left it and told the Spirit Woman to come back with something she might have more chance of understanding. So we proceeded with her reading for her future.

Just before finishing the reading the same Spirit Lady returned, but this time she was dancing around me, accompanied by her rendition of '*Aye, Aye, Aye, Aye, like you very much*'.

I explained what was happening and asked again:

'Are you sure that you know nothing of Carman Miranda? I know that it's well before your time, it's almost before mine!'

I told her it was Carman Miranda who used to sing this song, and that she was very famous for it. The girl pulled a face at me - as most of them do – then I said that she wore lots of fruit on her head, apples, grapes...

Suddenly her eyes widened and she shrieked:

'Yes! Yes! It's my auntie, she grew *oranges & lemons* and she had a black straw hat full of fruit - she was very proud of her hat!'

The girl started to get upset and told me how sorry she was that she didn't understand the first time. I said,

'Don't be silly! I don't mind as long as we get it sorted, and that spirit get through in the end. That's all I care about! Not only do they have to get something that I can understand and translate to you, but it must also be able to be understood by you.'

* * *

Somerset;
Recorder Girl

A Spirit Man materialised soon after a nice girl sat at my table. He stood beside her. I asked him who he was. He said that he used to teach her the recorder in her junior school. When I told her this, she just laughed and laughed.

She could not believe that it was him and that he could come to her.

I told her that he was telling me where she used to sit in class. I described what clothes he would normally wear and the fact that he liked her and that he could never get her to play the recorder properly.

I also had to explain that he was demonstrating to me her ability as a recorder player by way of sticking his fingers in his ears and laughing. But all of this was done without menaces and with great humour.

He told me that she would get very upset by her continual

failure at playing the recorder. She said everything I told her was quite correct and that the music teacher felt sorry for her but couldn't help. When the time came for the school concert they wouldn't let her play.

She looked back on this time with happiness and had no regrets.

* * *

Surbiton;
Man at Surbiton

A very tall and broad-shouldered man asked my son Anthony to book him in for a consultation. He appeared to be a very dominant person. Whilst he walked off towards Sainsbury's I said to Anthony,

'Has he booked in?'

'Yes, why?' he replied.

'Oh, I thought, he is either going to be great or horrible!'

When his time was due he promptly arrived and sat down. I picked up the cards and started to shuffle them. Whilst I was doing this an image of a grave-yard started to form. It was well kept. A Spirit man at my side was showing me this; he told me that he looked after these people.

I asked the man who had sat down in front of me whether he knew of any person that lived near a graveyard.

'I'm being shown a house and a well kept graveyard, and the person that looked after this is standing beside you. He seemed to love this place. Was he the caretaker or something along those lines? He is a small man dressed in black.'

The big man opposite me asked, 'Did he say anything at all?'

'No,' I said 'but he is making me aware that he intends to stand here and make sure I do your reading correctly. But I am sure he'll intervene if we do go down a wrong path. Do you know this man?'

'Yes,' he said, 'he's my father. He used to be a vicar in the countryside not far from here.'

I said 'we had better make a start, as he might interject as we went on'

Half-way through the reading the man's mobile phone went off, and unfortunately I overheard a woman on the other end... Nagging!

'Did you get this, did you get that?' she demanded.

You could see by the grimace on his face that this was an unpleasant phone call, but he was used to it.

Just after the call ended his father jumped in and said,

'She'll be gone in six months time; he will be out of it!'

With that a glimpse of the future appeared in my head. I saw and heard doors banging and it was the big man in front of me banging them and shouting.

I told him what his father had said and shown me. He just looked at me.

I said, 'I'm sorry, but I had to tell you. And boy! Haven't you got a temper?'

He smiled and said, 'Yes, when driven.'

'Yes,' I said, 'your father did show me!'

I gave him his tape. He shook my hand and left.

I could have fancied him myself.

* * *

Basingstoke;
Cut Ginger

A young girl sat before me with her brilliant ginger hair. Oh, it was lovely!

As I was shuffling her cards in preparation for her reading I remarked upon her hair, saying that I liked it very much.

Suddenly I had a vision of when she was about five or six years old. I was standing behind her but just to one side, with a friend of hers on the other. I could see her face reflecting in the mirror and her beautiful ginger hair shimmering in the light.

It was then that I saw a pair of scissors being raised up towards her head. Her friend started hacking off her hair in big chunks from the base. Chunk after chunk after chunk fell to the floor, colouring the floor with flashes of copper. This madness only lasted for a few minutes.

It was only after the deed had been done and calm had overtaken the pair of children that the realisation of what had taken place formed.

Fear, panic and terror set in and both she and her friend attempted to gather the hair from the floor and glue it to her head in big clumps before her parents found out.

I looked up and remarked,

'You've got such lovely hair, why on earth would you want to cut it all off and then stick it to your head?'

She looked at me aghast and

14

wanted to know how I knew. I relayed what I had seen to her.

She was gob-smacked!

'You are always looked after and watched out for in your life by your guides, helpers or angels,' I added.

* * *

Dolphin Nursery;
Still Birth

A big fat lady sat down and straight away I could see her putting food continually into her mouth. The cause was the emotional turmoil she was suffering under, and as it never left her she just put more and more food in her mouth. It was her guide that showed me this.

I dealt the cards whilst wondering how I could approach this very delicate subject during her consultation. As we progressed though the reading all of the emotional turmoil emerged in her cards.

At the end of the reading I held her hand and asked her why she was trapped in this cycle of eating? She said it was due to her unhappiness, and that all this unhappiness was due to her having had a *still-born* child.

'The child will come back to you when you have another baby,' I said. 'It will be him!'

She couldn't believe what I was saying.

'Really?' she said, the tears streaming down her face.

'Yes' I replied.

I then proceeded to explain that sometimes Spirit is too quick to come back and that they can make a mistake - i.e. wrong marriage, country, and parents. So they leave us at this time until things change.

Wiping her tears away, she said,

'Well, I did have another baby boy not long after.'

15

I asked how old he was, and with that she pointed to a boy not far away.

'He's thirteen.'

'You have been suffering all of these years,' I said, 'and he has been with you all along!'

Bursting into tears again, she said she wanted to take psychic classes with me.

* * *

Kew;
Pub at Kew

The Landlady of a pub in Kew came to see me, at the recommendation of one of her friends. She invited me to attend her pub for 'Guy Fawkes Night' in my professional capacity. I agreed on one condition: that they plied me with an unlimited amount of tea!

Upon my arrival she asked me if she could be first, to which I agreed.

She mentioned terms and I said that if she could arrange for my Granddaughter and I to have dinner afterwards that would be quite satisfactory.

As soon as she took her seat, and before I even picked up my cards, the clairvoyance started. I found myself sat on a chair with a window to my right and my left hand on an empty bed. I didn't know why, but I was made to have another look around this room. Little of it seemed clear. I looked to my right and there was the window that I had previously seen the light green vinyl wing-backed armchair with my wrinkled hands resting on the arms and an empty bed with a walking stick leant against it.

Wrinkly Hands!!

I'm Old! This is me, I'm an old woman, and I'm in a nursing home.

I explained all of this to the Landlady of the pub.

'Yes! Yes!' she exclaimed, very surprised and excited.

I said, 'It's your Grandmother. She was in a nursing home.'

'Yes!' she replied. 'She was!'

With the recognition accepted and the energies built, I was suddenly thrown back into the light green chair in the nursing home and into the body of the old woman.

But this time I had company. Before me on the floor with her head on my lap was the Landlady of the pub, and I was stroking her head.

'Did this happen?' I said to the Landlady. 'Did she used do this to you?'

With tears in her eyes she replied, 'Yes, she did!'

After that it all got a bit confusing, because the old lady started to stroke my head. So there was I as the old lady stroking the Landlady's head, but having the old lady at the same time stroke mine!

I tried to explain to the Landlady what had gone on, with some eventual success, and it transpired that she used to visit her Grandmother and lay her head on her lap whilst being stroked by her Grandmother. But at the same time the Landlady would stroke her Grandmother's head.

This was confirmed by the old lady who made me laugh.

I relayed all the information I had gathered to the tearful Landlady. As I did so, she just cried some more and thanked me for bringing her granny to her, as it most definitely *was* her granny, and that she knew for sure.

We moved on to her future.

I was invited to her friend's pub the following week to work.

* * *

Oxford;
12 Men & True

My son and I took our Green Goddess - our green motor home - to an event in Oxford. I do prefer to do my readings outside of the van, so people will get a fresh look at things. I have tried to bring readings into the open for many years, as there are too many of these 'Gypsy Rose Lees' stuck in little caravans who just spout what they think you want to hear.

I'm very different; everything is in the open, honest and true, with nothing to hide. That is why you will always find me with my two chairs and my little table on the grass. Pending one factor that is… the usual changeable English weather – cold & raining.

So unfortunately, today I had to take shelter from nature and read in the van. Whilst warming my hands, I noticed through the window that for some unknown reason there were a lot of women gathering outside, waiting for their own reading, whilst taking it in turn to sit on our spare chairs. @nthony, my son, was looking after them very well, but when they came in one by one I still had to hold their hands to warm them up so they could shuffle the cards.

Obviously they weren't being looked after well enough!!

I remember one woman; I dealt the cards and told her that in her house was a legal letter. She said no, that wasn't right, so I shuffled again and saw courts and legal papers.

'No!' she said; so I shuffled again…

'The fact of the matter is that you do have legal things!'

'No,' she said; 'but everything else you've given me is right.'

So I went ahead and did her future.

Three hours later she came back and said, 'that legal thing, would it be jury service?'

I held up my hands and said, 'I rest my case, m'lud!'

Oxford;

The Girl with Two Shadows

A woman of about twenty-something arrived - I'm not that good with ages. She had long dark brown hair and glasses, and she was very thin and cold.

As she came in a strange warm shadow accompanied her; it was full of love so I was not concerned. She sat down and so did this shadow.

As we progressed with her consultation I told her that just in the recent past there has been a big shock with tears and a lot of upset.

In her future I saw a man in a suit with a brief-case.

'I am at court, he is the judge... But I am not afraid, as he is nice.'

I then found myself touching possessions belonging to someone else. It was then that I told her someone was sat next to her, someone who loved her very much, and that he would stay with her for as long as she needed him.

She kept smiling a nervous smile.

As the reading came to an end I said to her:

'Mainly you are trying to sort out a lot of things at home.'

Afterwards she told me that her boyfriend had died the previous week and that the judge I had seen was the coroner. Also that both of them were moving in together at the time of his death, so she had all of his things in their new home, but that she was going to give up the new home as it just wasn't right any more...

She left accompanied by her loving shadow.

I did all I could for her; I still often think of her.

* * *

Oxford;

Is she any good?

Her friend came in and sat down. Nice girl, fair hair. Like the previous client, hands blue from the cold, and a lack of being *'properly looked after'*.

She looked out the window of the motor home and said,

'Good, she's crying! We were very worried about her; thank you for helping.

She had her cards read, which she was very happy about, and left.

Unbeknown to me, the girl and Anthony had a deal; she had said,

'Is your mum any good? Because I've just paid Gypsy Rose Lee for a three-minute rubbish reading and I've a good mind to ask for a refund!'

Anthony said, 'well if you do have a consultation and if you are not happy with anything at all you will get a full no-quibble money-back guarantee!'

When she left I saw him offer the money back, and she said 'no'

When I found out about all of this afterwards, I thought it was funny. But I'm glad I didn't know about beforehand, because it would have put me on the spot, and my nerves might have let me down.

* * *

Oxford;

The end is not nigh

The next lady came in and again, like her predecessors she was very cold.

For her I saw the ending of a big problem in her life, but when she saw the death card she went into a complete panic.

'Is that my cancer back?'

'No,' I said, 'that's the death of *it*! And don't bring it back to you by thinking otherwise. Just shut the door on it!'

Well that made her year, she was so happy! But before she left I said,

'So what do you all do? I know you work together and that you are all in a hurry,' - they had sat waiting for each other for two hours.

'Nurses,' she said, 'and we were all due back on duty a while ago. I thank you from all of us.'

I sat for a few moments and said my thanks to 'head-office'. I opened the door of the van only to find that it had got very dark and it was now 10 pm. We had dinner and retired for the night.

A very confused 'Gypsy Rose-Lee'.......

The very next morning whilst we were having breakfast outside basking in the morning glory, Anthony started to chuckle and said to me,

'I think somebody may be wondering where their weekend business has gone!'

As I looked up I could see the figure of 'Gypsy Rose-Lee' and her two enchantingly attractive daughters, both sporting 'Croydon face-lifts' and big silver hoop earrings, but alas without the parrots swinging from them; they are commonly, yet lovingly referred to as 'Chavs'. All three were wearing lovely green welly boots.

What an attractive sight first thing of a morning!

All three got closer and closer, and then just stopped some meters from our stall. They stared, snarled, and stormed off back to their caravan, which was adorned with the usual billboards purporting Gypsy-Rose-Lee to be the seventh daughter of the seventh daughter of gypsies... well, you know the story!!

Camden Town;
'Should she or shouldn't she?'

A lady and a young girl of about fifteen or sixteen years came to me. The lady said to me fairly harshly:

'Are you any good?'

'I've no complaints so far,' I replied.

With that she said, 'This is my daughter's money and I don't want it wasted.'

'I do understand,' I said. 'If your daughter is not satisfied she will of course get a full refund.'

'Yes,' she said, and beckoned her daughter to sit.

The mother thought that she was just going to stand behind and listen to her daughter's very private reading.

'There's a good pub over there,' I remarked to the mother. 'And lots of cafes, and stalls to look at. She will be about thirty minutes.

Her mother protested and protested. I explained that I would be picking things up from her and that this would not be fair to her daughter, as it was her reading after all.

'She will be fine!' I said, and eventually the girl and I persuaded her to move off.

On reading the girl's cards I could see that she was very fond of a young boy. I could also see that she was in two minds as to whether to give him sex or not. I then went on to describe her kitchen, and things being thrown from one side of it to the other as she got very angry with her mother. She agreed that this did happen.

'There is a man that you feel you can talk to,' I said, 'and you like each other. He is a fisherman and he is very good with maths - I also see him using a calculator.'

She looked very shocked and said that it was her mother's ex-boyfriend.

'You can talk to him privately without your mother knowing,' I said, 'and he will give you very good advice.'

The funniest thing that I said to her was:

'If you have a question you should say it quickly now, because your mother has been running in and out of the other stalls pretending to look at things and trying to listen!' We both found this very funny, how desperate she was to listen to this reading.

So far the young lady had written everything down, and her question was: should she or shouldn't she have sex with this boy, as she was still a virgin.

I said to her, 'Don't write this down in case it should fall into enemy hands!' and we both laughed. The mother was at the next stall so I whispered to the girl, 'You have already made your mind up, so use a condom and be grown up about it.'

The mother re-appeared and said to the girl, 'Well, what do you think?'

'Very good!' the girl replied, 'and I'll come back again.'

As the girl arose from her chair the mother looked at me and demanded to know what her daughter had said.

I replied in a loud voice, 'That is between me, the client, head-office and nobody else!'

But whilst they were walking away, I overheard her say to the girl,

'Well, what did she say?'

With that the girl looked around at me and I gestured to her that she should eat the paper that she wrote the reading on to destroy the evidence...

* * *

Camden Lock;
From Gunslinger to Pussycat

A man stood in front of me and just stared with his hands on his hips as if ready for the draw in a gun fight. Sound then came from his lips and he said,

'What is a brief reading?' He appeared very aggressive and agitated, and he was now pacing in front of me still with his hands on his hips.

I rejoined with: 'A brief reading is brief!'

I am naughty but I was trying to lighten the situation.

He pulled the chair up, sat down and instructed me to 'go on then!'

I had my cards in my hands trying to make up my mind if I really wanted my aura infested with him.

'What do you expect from this?' I asked him.

'I don't know! Why aren't you doing it?' he demanded.

My reply was that I was trying to make up my mind whether I would read for him or not.

He could not believe what I had just said to him. He was certainly taken aback, as his mouth just fell open.

I continued by saying: 'I don't need your money, and I still don't know whether to read for you or not.' But something told me to do it.

So we proceeded. His first card told me all I needed to know!! How he was so highly strung and mixed up in the head.

He looked at me aghast, he was so shocked, and whilst stumbling for an answer, 'Yes, that's right!' just fell out.

'That is what I was picking up from over there' I said.

Then he replied, 'Oh, I am sorry if I seem aggressive, I don't mean to be.'

During the next portion of his consultation I said that head-office was telling me about the mother of his child and that she gave him lots of problems.

'Yes!' he retorted. 'And that's what doing my head in.'

I then informed him that there would be a man from the council, and that he shouldn't be aggressive towards this person as he would be able to help.

'But remember, you must change your attitude towards people, otherwise they won't want to help you.'

Moving on I could see that there would be a big change in six weeks' time. I could see him selling his council house. He was doing a deal which is called 'back-to-back' - he was taking the money back to Brazil for a while and that he would then return to England.

He confirmed that this was all correct and that he would come back to see me.

* * *

Strawberry Hill;

Over the Strawberry Hill or just a small problem?

A woman in her mid-years sat before me, and the first thing I could see straight away was a man's droopy penis and a pair of testicles. I didn't mention it to her at first; I just put it to one side (pardon the pun).

We started the reading and her first card was the lovers, but all I could see was arguing and bickering between her and a man. I said to her,

'He is a nice man, but he has a penis problem.'

'Yes!' she said, 'he does, and this is what all of the arguing is about.'

'Tell him to get to the doctors and get some Viagra,' I said, 'and if you do this I can see a better future for you both. And if he won't go tell him that I saw it, and he's got to go!'

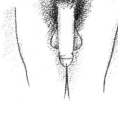

Before she left I remarked to her that this was the second penis problem that day, and that maybe the council was putting something extra in the water.

'Are you over-populated in Strawberry Hill?' I asked.

25

I found it very strange: to be staring at a man's penis and testicles that I had never met before. It's good that I have a sense of humour!

* * *

Somerset;
The Little Girl

A lady with two sons of about ten and eleven years old arrived. The boys sat a few metres away and their mother sat opposite me in the 'hot seat'. She seemed a very nice person but she was quite stiff.

Her first card was 'Great Happiness' for the coming week. Then I saw a small child. I asked her if there was a small girl around either here or in the family. She said no.

I tried to move on but I couldn't, I just kept being dragged back to the first card. I asked the woman if she had a child that had passed on, as there was definitely one here. The lady stiffened up immediately and was frightened to believe what I said.

I went on: 'The happiness next week will be caused by you seeing her.'

By now the lady is looking at me in disbelief.

'This little girl that's on my left side is telling me that you will be doing your hair, and in the mirror you will see her. It will be very quick, but please don't look for it or you will stop it from happening.'

At this moment the girl started to flap the bottom of her dress at me. At first I thought at first it was the dress itself that she wanted to make a point of, but actually it turned out to be the colour. The dress was in two layers, the bottom layer was fuchsia pink and the top was bright pink. I was told to look at my colouring pencils which I happened to have on my table. I picked two up and said,

'She is going on about these two colours, one being fuchsia pink and the other bright pink. Does this mean anything to you?'

'Yes,' the lady replied. 'I purchased some bathroom towels last week, one of each colour, and the boys over there were arguing that they were just too girlie for them!'

'She is telling me about the towels as proof that she was in the shop with you all and that she knows all about them,' I said.

With that the little girl went on tip-toes and gently brushed my cheek. As I was telling the lady what she had done, I saw the little girl walk around to her mother, and just as I finished telling her of what the girl had done to me, the lady said,

'I know she has just done the same to me.'

'It was so gentle; it was like being stroked by a peach!' I said.

My son Anthony heard it all as he was on the next stall, and his eyes just filled up.

I said to the lady, 'Thank you very much, I found it an honour to meet your daughter.'

The little girl stroked my cheek again to say thank you.

I did a funny thing: I looked down and said 'thank you' to her.

And she left with her mother.

* * *

Somerset;
Pretty Wo-Man

She sat down with her nice nails, nice hair and a well made-up face, but still something just wasn't right. She shuffled the cards and I laid them out. As I looked into the cards I knew that something strange was going on.

'You are very artistic, like in the way you make your face up and do you hair, I told her. 'I had a friend like you. She was a drummer.'

As we progressed with her consultation I told her that she was a teacher and that she wanted to do public speaking but was too shy to do it.

'Yes' she said.

I then said that my friend was like that before HE had the operation.

She still would not face the fact that I knew she was a man.

She had the same partner for twenty-eight years, which I think is most commendable.

She was my first transvestite.

* * *

Strawberry Hill;
The bridge away from troubled waters

As a rather rotund lady took the 'hot seat' I had visions of her naked atop a massage table.

I said to her, 'When you were having a massage you had a very spiritual experience which you have never spoken of but you have never forgotten. During that massage you were very sad and did not want to be here anymore. In other words you wanted to die. Also during this moment you saw a very large black lady on the other side of a bridge. She said to you, "You can come if you wish, but we would like you to stay".'

So I told the lady what her guide was trying to say, that she

must stay here and learn her lessons.

'Yes,' she said, 'I knew to have a reading from you.'

I saw that she played around with tarot cards, but I said to her,

'Please don't do this until you have sorted your personal problems out.'

Somerset;

No title

A nice young lady sat down. The feeling that I immediately got from her was a lot of shock. I told her,

'This person that caused the shock is a male, but it would appear that there are two males in your life. I also feel that you would love to leave your house and possibly 'run away' because of what happened.

I was then played a video in my head; I could see a man coming towards her and it was somebody she knew. He was all over her for a while.

It suddenly hit me; I looked up at her and said, 'You were raped.'

The video then continued, and once he had done what he wanted she just stood there, frozen to the spot and feeling like jelly. She was in a state of sheer disbelief, not just because she had been raped, but because of the person who had done it!

Once again I looked up at her and said,

'You were raped, but it was your brother-in-law, wasn't it?'

She just sat there with her eyes welling up, speechless, just nodding. She didn't speak for a while until the reading had finished.

It was at the end that she told me she didn't know whether to tell his wife and her husband - his brother - about it. I said that speaking about it would bring no gain for anybody, just more hurt and pain.

* * *

Somerset;
'Tell 'im to eff-off'!'

Another seeker sat down, she had a pretty face with a fair complexion. She shuffled the cards, but as the cards were being laid out a lot of upset became apparent. There was a relationship problem, a young man was playing her around, and she was all broken up inside with it.

My naughty dad suddenly came flying in and said,

'Tell 'im to eff-off, as 'e never will be no good to 'er!'

I did try to ignore it, but my Dad kept on and on about it, so with me being that I don't swear the 'F' word I had to write the letter 'F' on a bit of paper and show it to her. I told her what my dad had been like when he was here, and that he was just the same now that he was over there on the other side, but also that he is a very fair man, although alas he has got a very foul mouth.

At that she laughed and said that she agreed with my dad. My dad once again jumped in and remarked, 'this person will always

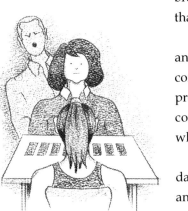

break your heart in two, he is just that sort.'

In her heart the girl knew this, and it appeared that I was just confirming her inner feelings. We progressed on with the part of her consultation about the future, which was a bit brighter.

As she left I apologised for my dad's behaviour but she laughed and retorted,

'No, I liked him!'

* * *

Bristol;

Chinese Customs

A Chinese man sat down before me. I did his reading, which wasn't too bad until we got to the last card.

'I do not understand this,' I said to him, 'but all I know is that it is something very religious and I have to stand and put two hands together and bow quite a lot, up and down. It is all connected to religion.'

At these words the blood drained from his face. 'I hope not,' he said, 'oh no!'

'What is it? I asked him. 'What is it I'm talking about? What does it all mean?'

'You do this to your forebears when they die,' he replied.

'I'm very sorry,' I said, 'but that is what I saw and I can't say otherwise to you.'

I must say, though, that he was impressed with his reading because my son Anthony overheard him recommending me to others close to our stall.

* * *

Bristol;

Death Becomes Her

A lady of more mature years, at least 65, sat before me. As I was doing her cards I was told by spirit that for years she had been having an affair with a man. I told her this and to my surprise she agreed! I couldn't believe it due to her age. I kept hearing a song repeating over and over:

'Tula-tula-lula-lula,
Tura-lula-lay,
Tura-tura-lula-lura,
Hush now don't you cry.'

It is called 'An Irish lullaby'.

After I'd sung that she sat bolt upright and said, 'My mother used to sing that to me in Ireland.'

I carried on 'She's telling me to tell you that you will receive a telephone call informing you that the wife of the man you are having an affair with will die.' At this she seemed very pleased.

We moved on to her future, after which she told me that she was very happy with her consultation, and left.

* * *

Wales;
Breakfast at Tiffany's

A very timid young lady took her place upon the throne opposite; as we proceeded with her reading it turned out to be quite an interesting consultation. But it soon became apparent that she was having an affair. She said it was 'just for fun'.

She was wearing quite a few rings on both hands. I was asked by spirit to touch just one ring; I didn't know why but I soon found out. It was the smallest one with a green stone inset.

When I did touch it, I felt that something was missing.

'What significance does this ring hold, and why do I feel that something is missing? I asked her.

She looked very surprised and very nervous.

She said 'the earrings that belong to this set are missing, and they had all been a present from my husband' She carried on by saying 'they might have been lost at a Bed and Breakfast during a secret assignation. And they were very, very expensive'

I finished by telling her that there was a very good reason why they had pointed this out to me and that if she kept on playing around, next time it might be her family and her home that she loses and not just her earrings.

* * *

Camden;
Manic Depressive

A young girl of twenty or so years approached me for her cards to be read. She seemed neither happy-nor sad. She was, just so.

During the reading I could see that she was on a small break; a little holiday and yet she was not in a happy state.

From the next card I could see that she was sorting things out on a short break; how strange. There was a big burden in her life that would go on for a long time and it came from her mother; in fact it was her mother that was, and always would be, the burden.

I could see all of this young lady's worry regarding her mother.

As her mother came forward in spirit, she imparted to me that she had been a manic depressive and that she had committed suicide. The young girl would always be looking over her shoulder expecting this illness to strike at her at anytime.

I reassured her that this would not happen, and so did her mother, but that she would go back to her university less fearful for the rest of her life.

God bless her.

* * *

33

Camden;

Drugs 'R' us

A tight-fitting-woolly-hat-wearing young man wanted a consultation.

As soon as he sat down I said to him, 'The police are after you!'

He ducked his head a little and looked around from left to right, very shifty-like, but slowly. Then he leant close to me and said,

'Have they been around asking questions?'

I replied, 'Just shuffle the cards and say nothing.'

It turned out that my first feelings were indeed correct and that the police were after him good and proper! I could see it all in the cards.

I told him that all of his so-called 'friends' would be stabbing him in the back and that in one week's time he would become a 'tea-bag'.

He looked at me oddly, and it was only when I said 'a tea-bag is full of holes' that he understood.

The rest of this reading is dangerous and very private, but I will add this: a couple of days later he telephoned me and said,

'Hi Collette, I'm now a 'tea-bag'.

I saw the 'tea-bag' over the next few months when he would come by for a reading, but after a few months he disappeared.

Maybe his 'friends' got him, or perhaps Her Majesty offered him an extended all-expenses paid holiday at *Her Majesty's Pleasure.*

He wasn't a bad person; he just took the wrong path along the way.

* * *

Camden;

The Witch Doctor

I was sat at my table enjoying the warmth of the sun whilst taking my time writing a letter to my granddaughter when I was overcast by a large shadow. I looked up expecting a big black cloud to have come between me and the sun, but to my surprise it wasn't a cloud at all. It was a big black man. He was huge; he was like a man mountain - but not of fat. The only way to do him proper justice would be to liken him to the black actor from a very good film called 'The Green Mile'.

He was reading one of the star sign birth charts that I was selling. I said to him,

'Oh, you are a Sagittarius?'

He looked up and with a wry smile replied, 'Yes - but you should know that!'

I laughed and said, 'No, I'm a clairvoyant and I use the cards, that's what I do'.

'Oh, what do you do with them?' he asked inquisitively. It was obvious that he wasn't long in this country.

I said, 'I tell a bit of your future.' He looked down and carried on reading his star-sign chart, but at the same time he was thinking about what I had just said. He looked up at me and said, 'Yes, you can indeed speak of the future.'

Going by what he said and what I was feeling, I felt sure that he was a medium or similar in his own country.

He sat down and said, 'I have a few minutes to spare.'

'Oh god, I hope I can do a good job for him!'

This was the first thing that went through my mind. He looked at me again and said, 'How is your son?'

'Which one?' I replied.

'The little one,' he said.

(*The little one was put through a glass security window by some animal for no reason at all, which I was still very upset about. My twenty-*

five-year old son, believe it or not, was perfectly all right).

The man thought for a minute and looked at me and said, 'This man is a bouncer at a club. He is very un-intelligent.'

I said, 'I think that fits the bill!'

So I did his cards. He was very pleased with what I said.

He then stood and said, 'I must go now but I will be back for a longer reading.'

I look forward to seeing him again; one medium to another.

How strange. And his reading was very strange, as he had to tell a lot of lies to stay in this country.

* * *

Camden;
The Aussie floor-layer; he'd lay anything…

A short, hard-working, honest man, who had never had his cards read, sat before me.

Before we touched the cards I said,

'There are people after you, not to beat you up or kill you though, just after you. Let's shuffle the cards and see what's going on…'

At first he was very distrusting of the reading, but it turned out that the people who were after him were the electricity and gas boards, a number of banks, the tax man, and many other people and organisations, all after money.

He took my card and shook my hand and said,

'Well, I thought all of this stuff was a load of rubbish. Thank you very much, Collette.' He left after kissing my hand.

Camden;

Wants Her Cake and Eat It....

A very pretty blonde girl sat down, she spoke English but still sounded foreign. It later turned out that she was from South Africa.

As we progressed with her consultation I informed her of a very imminent big change in her life.

'Yes' she said 'I'm going home' I also said that there is somebody quite close to you who you just want to say 'oh piss-off' and that I don't want you anywhere near me'

'Yes yes, it's true' I then said that I couldn't make up my mind if it's a woman or a man, as it keeps fluctuating and I don't quite understand it.

I suddenly saw that this person was a lesbian, and it was her 'landlady or landlord' you could say; but worse still, it was her cousin!

I said 'that families can be the worst kind of trouble you can get, due to the connec- tions, and that old sayings are often true;

'You can pick your friends - but not your family'

Before this young girl left she also confided in me that her cousin not only wanted to collect the rent from her, she also wanted sexual favours.

'Typical woman; wants her cake and eat it'

* * *

Camden;
The blind leading the blind....

A very cocky girl sat down, she seemed so sure of herself.

A real big I am.

As her reading continued I found her mind completely trapped, confused and in a mess, I relayed this to her, to which she retorted a resounding 'No!'

So we proceeded with her reading nonetheless, as I know that my guides/angels/helpers are never wrong; sometimes they struggle in getting their message understood by me, or I to the client, but we get there in the end.

So come the end she did indeed realise that in her head she was in a mess, but before we got to that milestone she remarked, all cocky like 'that she was surprised that I think that her head was in a mess as I am a psychiatric nurse and I know everything about people and I love to psychoanalyse people, I could sit here and talk to you all day to find out how you tick and I love doing this with the patients'

Oh dear I thought........ 'The blind leading the blind'

Before we parted I just had to say to her, 'but forgive me, perhaps you should spend some time sorting your own head out first and try to understand yourself, before you can possibly help anybody else.

Maybe your efforts should be turned more inwards, instead out outwards'

Please forgive me for being so open and straightforward.....

She left not as cocky as she arrived, but when she left I thought poor patients.

* * *

Camden;

It's a Posh Chinese, well dressed Affair.

As I am only human and not infallible to human errors, a lesson for me to take heed was when a young Chinese girl in Camden sat before me.

At Camden Lock I have a lot of foreign tourists visiting me and between us we can normally sort out the language barrier, well eventually anyway.

But on this particular day a very attractive young Chinese girl sat before me and I automatically and I admit wrongly, judged this book by its cover. I assumed she was lacking in a good standard of English.

Before her reading I held up the cards and saying very 'sloowwly' 'yooou shufflee thhee caarrds' and you could have blown me down with a feather after what came out of her mouth, her English was better than mine, better than the Queen's or Sir Trevor McDonald's.

This girl was more posh than Harrod's and Fortnum & Mason's put together.

She said in an awfully, awfully posh voice 'Oh, yes that would be no problem whatsoever, I'm sure that I could quite easily mange that'

Shocked and surprised I enquired as to the reason that she spoke with such a command, lexicon and elocution of the English language, she said that she attends a very expensive school in Kent, the one Princess Anne was sent to. Well I never, what a surprise, that certainly tore me off a strip.

As her consultation continued it turns out that she has just been in an affair with a very prominent lawyer, and that he had just finished it.

I could see all of this and all of the tears in her heart, I said to her;

'That you want to continue this affair but alas it will not'

At the end of her personal reading, she paid me a wonderful compliment, she said 'you are very good; you should not be working here, you should be at Covent Garden. If I take your card will you come to my school Kent? I'm sure we could smuggle you in?'

Well this appealed to my sense of humour; it would be just like the naughty girls at 'St Trinians' (films based on the work of cartoonist Ronald Searle)

I then said that I like working in Camden as it keeps my feet firmly on the ground.

* * *

Kingston;
A 400 year old Gypsy........ and still looking fit.

A woman in her prime (60 years) sat down and asked for a 'small reading'

I said; 'I don't know about that, but I do think that there is a dwarf clairvoyant just up the road a bit, and that you may get more joy of a 'small reading' there'

She looked a little stunned and confused at first but once I smiled and laughed she realised it's was only a joke.

As a consultation goes I could have gone on forever with her, if ever there was a perfect link this was it; I can only liken it to a 30mb broadband connection.

Description wise, I would say that she was over sixty, fit and very psychic, and she knew she was. So much so to the point that she knew that she should or could do what I do.

I got her past, present and future even though she only asked for a 'small reading'

After the reading she was telling my son how pleased she was with her reading and she then reeled back to me and said;

'You are absolutely spot-on with everything you said, you're a marvel'

With the link quickly reconnected I told her that she was from a gypsy background, and I could go back 400 hundred years and find her family of gypsies, 'Yes, Yes you are so right!' She said.

More than anything else, what I did not say because there was not time and my son had booked people in and I had a queue.

The thing was that I knew this woman before, when I was a gypsy traveller, and I was friends with her tribe.

It was a shock to me, as it was hundreds of years ago. Wow!!

* * *

Camden;
Japanese bowing

A Japanese young man approached me in Camden; he said that wanted to purchase my 'star sign' throw (cloth backdrop) that I had hung up as my display for my stall. I said 'no, that's mine and its part of my stall'

He looked disappointed. Tell me he said, 'what are these cards about?'

I tried to explain and said 'sit down and try' so he did.

He looked a bit scruffy, dyed blonde hair! Have you ever seen a Japanese man with dyed blonde hair? I thought it looked quite nice but I liked him anyway. After his reading and whilst the cards were still on the table he was on the telephone telling somebody about his reading in Japanese, he also wrote his reading out in that wonderful writing, he showed it to me.

During the consultation I told him that he currently has one piece of music that he will present to a record label and it will be successful, he said that he was in the music business. He liked his reading so much and it made him so happy he insisted on paying me *double*.

I stood up and clasped my hands together and bowed to him,

he reciprocated. Then I bowed to him, and he too I.

The other market traders just looked at us as if we were mad.

I will never forget him; he was about 27 years old.

I hope he made it......

* * *

Camden;
A woman I could not do....

A woman in a grey suit took the throne; she appeared to be a business lady. She shuffled the cards and laid them out; I knew she was in a rush, she was very stressed, tense and all jangled up inside, but I wouldn't let that hinder me. I tried to read the dealt cards but they just didn't feel right, so I asked her to re-shuffle them, as I looked at them they still didn't feel right, so once again I requested that she re-shuffle them which she did. She was so closed up; this was the tension coming out.

I was still not happy, and I said to her that I would not compromise my integrity, so madam I feel that we unfortunately do not 'gel-together' today.

She seemed upset I said to her don't worry it does happened, very rarely mind you. She said that she would come back another day because I am very honest.

I said if you wish I will be willing to try for you again someday and I gave her a refund.

* * *

Epson Races;
Where's one when you want one?

A coach load of gas fitters turned up at Epson races for a day's betting, drinking and whatever gas fitters do when they're not handling their pipes. After consulting for one man he returned to the coach and told the others, so bit by bit I read for quite a number of their party.

At about 5pm another gas man came wondering by, slightly worse for wear. I did a consultation for him, he was a nice man. As I was talking to him he suddenly held my hand, he then burst into tears. I called to my son Anthony to drag him off, only joking.... to get him some tissues.

So there we were, sat at my table and two chairs on the grass at the Epson Races, surrounded by stalls, vehicles and the 'donkeys' running around and around the track with hundreds of thousands of people screaming for their 'dobbin' to come first. There were many people milling around the various stalls all looking for a bargain, what must they have thought I was doing to this poor tearful man I have no idea.

He was full of apologies for his tears, he said 'I don't know why I am crying' I held his hand and replied that 'firstly I am a healer, so you would have got a lot of healing whilst sat there, as I have two main groups of Guides that work with me; I have my Healing Guides and my Clairvoyant Guides'

So when people sit before me my Clairvoyant Guides help me with what you are here for and expect, but what people don't realise is that they receive a lot of healing in the process from my Healing Guides.

'Many people say they never want to leave my table as they feel so at peace and at home here, and that sometimes is because of the healing that takes place and that your channels are also opened, thus opening up what you have been burying'

'It's like a *buy-one-get-one-free* but nobody knows'

With tears still streaming down his face, he said 'I didn't realise that I was still grieving, my auntie passed away a while ago, and I thought that I had sort of got over it. But I am now worried sick about my Mother'

Until he met me that is....

I told him that he had nothing to worry about regarding his mother and his near future looked fine.

He left feeling much better and much lighter.

It was funny really he had been hanging around and looking at me for most of the day, he said that 'he was just passing by', you know......

I feel that the little of the 'Dutch courage' (drink) he thought he needed to approach me was possibly a little too much.

* * *

Epson Races;
You are going along way-away to a far off land....

A good looking man sat in front of me, he had very dark hair and appeared to be very fed-up, and he said that he only wanted a short reading so we started.

I told him that his life as it was now was concluding. I then saw the moon and a suitcase, I then saw the same suitcase being clutched by him whilst trying to negotiate the bathroom window. I said to him that 'he would leave his house very quickly, you are there one day and gone the next. You tell nobody that you are going; and then you're just, gone. And, you are taking a lot of money with you'

'Yes!' he said, I'm totally gobsmacked that....that.....as he paused...

That you can do that! How can you do that?'

I replied 'I don't know, it's just what I do'

I carried on 'gobsmacking him by telling him that was also buying his council flat and selling it the same day in a back-to-back deal.

(Something that is questionably legal, but carries on quite a lot)

And that he's then going to move to Australia.

The rest of his cards were good. So it was all a good things for him to do. My son and I watched him walk back to his car, he was over the moon, shouting and carrying on. Throughout the day he persuaded a number of his friends to come and have a reading as well.

But before the day was out he returned to see me, and said 'I'm still gobsmacked at how you know these things' I said 'I am as well, sometimes I know things, I see things and get scared it's wrong, so I don't always say. But with you I knew it was right, it was so strong' he said 'god bless you, and don't stop doing this work, you have given me a light at the end of my tunnel'

Just prior to walking away he came over and kissed me on the cheek.

I like reading for men; as I get a lot of kisses.

* * *

Epson Races;
The bruised skating Healer...

A very stocky man sat down, the type you may not want to meet in a darkened alley at a first glance. But this one was full of light and surrounded by so much loving energy, his aura was beautiful it was gold and silver all intertwined.

He was such a beautiful soul; I was certainly amazed to find him at a racecourse.

As the consultation started I saw his children in the cards and the fact that he was a lovely family man and that his wife and children love him very much. I then embarrassed him accidently, by telling him that he was every woman's dream of a man.

I suggested that he should attend his local Spiritualist Church; he looked at me in astonishment and enquired as to why? I said to him 'you are a wonderful healer, although you don't know it yet and you should be working in this field' he said that he didn't know where one was so I asked where he lived, 'Stevenage in

Hertfordshire' he replied.

'Well blow me down! I used to live there, do know the ice rink?'

'Yes of course' he chuckled, 'I go there every weekend with the kids. The kids love it but I keep falling over and I've the bruises to prove'

I told him that I campaigned for a year for that I was on the local radio station Chiltern fm and in the newspapers every week, and I had to gather a petition of thousands.

He laughed and said 'I have heard of you, but I didn't realise it was the same woman 20 years later, and in a completely different part of the world '

We shook hands and we parted.

* * *

Bristol;
Steve's £80,000 'accounting error'.....

Wow, Wow, this gorgeous man of about 6'3", blonde hair, broad shouldered wearing jumper and jeans asked for a reading.

As the consultation progressed it was becoming apparent that there was a real big problem in his life and it was concerning legal documents regarding property, court proceeding and money investments.

It turned out he was losing £80,000 on a property deal as his accountant, was, let's say 'managing the finances, but only in the accountants favour' *(to put it bluntly he was being stitched up by his accountant)* and it was all connected to property in Spain.

I can mention no more of this reading, but I will say that I have been asked by Steve to travel to Spain and stay in his home so that I could consult for him and some close friends.

I liked him very much, so probably best if I stay away.

* * *

Dunfermline;
A little help from a friend...

Whilst talking to a friend of mine called Stuart, who has a health food shop in Bridge St, Dunfermline, Scotland. A customer came in and approached the front counter; I stood aside so that he could be served.

He had dark hair; and was about 30-40 years of age. Stuart appeared to know him well. As they were talking the gentleman took off the rucksack from his back to place inside his purchases, he then struggled to re-fasten the rucksack of which he became embarrassed about.

Seeing that he was wearing a wedding ring I joked that he should get his wife to carry some of the shopping.

Suddenly I was taken by surprise as I heard from behind me a Scottish woman's voice say; 'Tell him that I am helping him to carry his load'

I looked around and said 'sorry love, what was that?' expecting a woman to be standing there as it was so clear, there was nobody there.

The voice then repeated 'Tell him that I am helping him to carry his load'

I am sorry, I did not have to courage to tell him as I was not doing a consultation at the time and it came out of the blue I did not feel comfortable to say, as the man wouldn't be expecting anything like that.

But I did tell Stuart after the man left the shop. Stuart just stopped dead and looked at me and said 'Oh, my god Collette. He lost his wife just two months ago to cancer'

At this time Stuart and I were doing a deal for him to stock my meditation cds in his shop. I said to Stuart 'next time you see that man please give him the 'Nature's Spell mediation cd for free, and he will meet his wife whilst doing it'

Greenford;
Uncomfortable with her Step-Dad......

A young woman from Lincoln looked on eagerly as I described her father who died and I told her that she used to get him milk. As she put her hand to her mouth in shock horror I moved on.

I started to pull a face with my eyes squeezed tight whilst swivelling my eyes from side to side, up and down. I asked 'who is this person that does this, and makes you feel uncomfortable?'

She said 'that's my step dad'

'He does not like you, does he?' I stated.

'No' she said.

You and your mum like each other and you get on very well, and you both go out together. But your step father is jealous of this isn't he? She looked down to her hands and agreed.

'Try to involve him more and he might stop hating you' I said. She just looked up glumly and disbelieving raised her eyebrows.

After I finished explaining that it was her dead 'real father' that was saying all of this, she thought a while, and replied, 'yes, I can see it now. I understand why my step father and I don't get on, and that it's not necessarily me he doesn't like. It's that fact of being pushed aside and left out that he doesn't like'

I suppose with her being only 16 it's possibly a bit much for her to work out for herself as she has enough to deal with being a teenager.

* * *

Greenford;
Vanity......

A young man of Indian origins came for a consultation, during which I told him;

'You wish to get out of a situation that you are in'

'Yes' he said.

I then said 'that he was also not happy in his current relationship', I told him that he is in the middle of some 'buy-to-let' property deal.

'Yes' he said with a look of shock on his face, 'both are true'

I was a bit worried to mention what I could see next, but nevertheless, me being me *'if I'm shown it, I give it'*

I was being shown that he liked dancing, and he kept looking in the mirror at himself dancing. He thought he was great!

I had to explain to him that if *I'm shown it, I have to give it* and that I'm shown things for a reason. His face was so funny, as he wasn't too sure what private little secret I was going to come out with!

I explained that the reason I was being shown this about his dancing was to provide proof your grandfather watches you doing this. And your grandfather tells me that he had to pick on that something that nobody else knows about for exact confirmation.

The young man said that he does dance in the mirror and that he thinks he's great. I didn't want to disappoint him, so I didn't mention that I wouldn't want him as my dance partner.

As the reading progressed I could see in another card that he is very artistic.

'Do you paint I asked?

'No' he replied,

'But I am very artistic with my beard; I think it's a work of art, don't you?'

As he stood there caressing it, tenderly. As if it was an injured dog.

Whilst trying to stop myself from choking I pleasantly smiled and moved very swiftly on, as I wasn't there to give my personal opinions upon his facial coiffure skills.

He was a nice person just slightly misguided and very, very vain.

Ealing;

There are many paths to my father's house; but all lead there.

Young lady called Kara, sat down. Very quickly a ghost/spirit/angel loved one pointed out her arms to me, I told her 'what I am seeing and how he helped her when she was self harming, and he tells me that it's all up and down your arms'

'Yes' she said 'this is true' and pulled up her sleeves to show me. I must admit I was shocked, but I didn't show it.

I tried to explain to young Kara who this person was stood here, I described how he had helped her out whilst he was alive, and that he is now showing me a path that had a lot of mess on it. And that he had straightened it out for her then set her on the right pathway.

After describing his broad shoulders, black clothes and that he was a nice gentleman as in really gentle. I then said 'You thought of him like a father figure'

'Yes' she said; with tears running down her cheeks. 'I know who that is'

'He tells me that he has been encouraging you lately to go to university' I said as I looked over my half rimmed spectacles at her.

'Yes' she sniffed 'I have just applied to study social work. I smiled and replied 'that she will be the best person for the job as most of them don't have a clue about the realities of life and that is what universities cannot teach you'

His message to you I told her 'Is that he will be with you every step of the way, even in the lectures with you.

She stood up from her chair and looked at me with tears of loss, regret, happiness and most of all understanding, she then shook my hand and said 'I will see you next year Collette'

* * *

Esher Fair;
*'I'm not being rude, but do **Shut up!**'*

'Hello, my name is Lynda' this lady said gushing as she sat down.

'Err... Hello' I replied as I looked up, a little stunned by this lady being so forthright.

Immediately I said; 'I am sorry if you think I'm rude, but can you please be quite and say nothing'

I said this because straight away I could see that she would tell me everything about her, unfortunately there are many people like this and she was one of the worst types. Trusting, trusting, and trusting some more.

Shame really, as these are the dream clients for the Gypsy-Rose-Lee's of this world.

Moving along swiftly, she was about 50 years young, well turned out in jeans and a blouse. She also had long flowing hair with nice grey bits running through and to top it off she was a jolly nice person.

I requested of her to 'just say yes, or no; and no more. Agreed? Without saying a word she looked at me, smiled and nodded. I returned the smile and said 'shall we begin then?' again she nodded but this time more quickly with a big smile and a glint in her eyes; pleasingly, she kept silent.

I said to her 'I am being shown a house, a nice house. Spirit is also showing me that you have a garden and there is a green door to the side of your house. But what is strange, is that, although you love your house, you feel that your Spirit/energy is all, ...well, the way I see it is that you feel all squashed when you walk out through the doorway of your house. It's more so when you feed the birds in your garden isn't it? I see you looking all around you as if you are in fear'

I did quite know where this was going, until I saw one of the curtains move in the house next door, and the sound of laughter coming from the same house. Except for it wasn't a happy laughter, it was mocking.

I looked at the lady sat before me and said, 'Lynda, the neighbours all around you really don't like you do they?' 'No' she said all upset, 'the reason is that they just don't understand you, do they?' 'And that they think you are a 'bit weird' and 'witchyfied' don't they? I softly asked her.

'Yes, that's right' she said, nodding with tears in her eyes.

I then said to her that 'All this makes you feel very lonely, but you are always aware of the lovely ghost in your bedroom, aren't you?

The one you frequently see in the dressing table mirror; then you don't feel so alone do you?'

Her face was a picture, eyes popped out; I said 'you often wondered if you were imagining this didn't you?

'Yes' she said.

'Sometimes people imagine others out of loneliness' I told her.

I carried on saying that 'I am being told that they will try to sort out your neighbours for you, and I have some good news for you, there is some love coming for you. It is in the sixth card which means it should be about two months away, please don't look for it as you will mess it all up.

Good luck to you and Spirit thank you for feeding the birds, and I will see you next year.

* * *

Esher Fair;
Washing Line........

A pretty young lady sat. I asked her to shuffle the cards, as she spoke she had an accent, so I enquired as to her origins, 'Canada' she replied, when she had finished shuffling I asked her to choose her cards. Whilst she was doing this I looked over toward the green grass surrounding the church and then my eyes wandered over to the road, and there before me strewn across this road from one side to the other was a washing line, I had to laugh, as there was all this washing pegged out white sheets, towels. All white her guide was telling me, all white.

I relayed all of what I was seeing to her, she looked at me....let's say a little odd. That is until I said to her that 'At home in Canada, you have a lot of dirty washing to sort out on your return, don't you? But I'm told that it will get done, and I'm also told to tell you once and for all.

She looked at me and said 'this is impossible, that you know all of this!' I said 'no-no, not me, it's your guide that knows all, not me. He knows all about you and the situation and the fact that you don't think that it can be sorted. But it can'

I then did her future. It ended up, a little cleaner shall we say. And everything came out in the wash.

* * *

Esher;
Stu-pot Stuart....

For those of you who don't come from the 1960's or from England, he was a 60's radio DJ, quite successful and he still looks good. He was the compare for the day at this little charity event, and part of his day's duties were to be the auctioneer of goods and services donated by local people and businesses, so we thought it to be a good idea as it was for charity to put copies of all of my meditation cds, a pack of tarot cards and a Clairvoyant consultation all up for auction, in other words, me for free! Ha-ha.

We thought it were great fun all of these people bidding like mad, in the end a young man got me. He promptly came to find out what time I could fit him in, so arranged we became.

When he returned I beckoned him to sit, and no sooner than he had sat, a lady from spirit arrived and stood by his side. She was a little on the chubby side, her jet black hair was streaked with grey running through and tied in a bun. She was wearing a black crotched shawl. Along with a grey skirt, a greyish blouse. I got that she was hard working and proud of it; I also sensed a great honesty with her also. Although she had this tough exterior, she had much love. Not soppy love.

She was fantastically precise with her information, she said for me to tell him that we came from fishing family, in Cork, Ireland, and we were there during the potato famine of 1845-1851. The only way we survived it was through fishing. The young man was very happy about this, he said, 'I have been told this by my family as well; exactly that!'

I remarked, whilst trying to do some mental arithmetic 'that she must be something like your great, great, great, great, great, great grandmother, or thereabouts. And she asks me; well more like instructs me to tell you that she is with you all of the time'

I smiled at him and said 'always remember if a medium cannot tell you correctly the past and present, why on earth should you believe what they tell you about the future!!!! Therefore it proves

that I'm not going to tell you a load of old rubbish, doesn't it?'

We proceeded with his future whilst his great, great, great, great, great, great grandmother, or thereabouts with her arms folded. Stood over us making sure I got everything right and proper, for she would not have it any other way.

He left slightly bemused and dumbfounded. Just the way I like it. I'll be seeing him again!

* * *

Clapham;

He's as cold as ice............Oh, but what a lovely man....

A really nice healer friend of mine calls me in sometimes for a consultation. This was the last visit I made to him. He tried to shuffle the cards, but being partially sighted this sometimes it's difficult for him, as he was shuffling them in his own way I started to see a building before me, all of the bricks were covered in ivy. As I looked further I noticed that the ivy had a mouth and it started talking, how weird.

I carried on watching the ivy for a while, and it was then I noticed that behind the ivy was a man, and he was using the ivy to hide his true self, and his real intentions. It was his true intentions to get rid of Reg and run this church his way, but poor Reg had put so much work and his life into the church so that it can provide a good place for people to come for peace and solace.

I said to Reg that 'spirit are saying that it's your work that's important and what you do for people, not where you do it that matters' All of a sudden the picture changed and the atmosphere was beautifully calm, serene and full of peace, I was transported into a big marble hall with marble pillars; many centuries past.

Once again the vision changed, but to be replaced by two large hands, they were marble like and ice cold, yet surrounded by a beautiful ethereal intense blue light. I conveyed this to Reg, he smiled and said 'I know exactly where you are Collette' I replied 'thank god for that as I don't'

He then said 'that when he does his healing work, he works with an old surgeon and that is why he is showing his hands; the hands of his craft. And I always see's the blue light, when we start' Reg then went on to say that 'the surgeon is from ancient times and the marble is where the seat of learning was'

As the consultation progressed I was now looking at a penis, I thought it belonged to a younger male and not Reg, not being a connoisseur on penis' myself, ha-ha; I just go on feelings and not that of the penis. But how do I tell this lovely old person what I am seeing, well there's only one way, and as you know me by now yes, you've got it!

'Straight from the shoulder'

Reg I said, 'who is connected to your house has a 'willy-problem' and it's not you, but connected to your house in some way, and in white sheets' 'Ahhh' he said raising one eyebrow, 'you are spot on again, it's my grandson, he's in hospital and today he's having an operation and they have to put a sort of wire thing up his penis, I think it's to get to his heart' said Reg, squirming a little in the chair.

'Oooo, rather him than me' I replied, whilst wincing.

'Now I know why the surgeon showed his hands Reg, but why are they are so ice cold?

Reg replied, 'that's just what my healing is like, ice cold. A lot of people mention it'

'Well' I said 'as long as it works, it doesn't matter how it happens'

As the consultation ended I closed by saying 'put the kettle on Reg and get the biscuit out, and don't worry about that horrible man at the church we will find a place for you to work if we put our heads together'

* * *

Cambridge;
Talking to walls? Each to their own, I suppose.........

Whilst doing a man's cards, I was continually being played a video in my head; it was of this man sat in front of me. In the video all I could make out was that he kept going to the back of his house all throughout his future reading.

Most odd behaviour I thought!

He just kept running to the back of his house in a mad panic but then returned to the front quite calmly. I asked if he lived in Norfolk as I felt that I was there. 'No' he said 'not far though, I live in Harwich which is in the next county'

I had to ask him, I explained that 'Spirit keeps showing me that you keep running to the back of the house and talking to a wall, and then walking back to the front? And then something happens, which makes you run to the back of the house and you then talk to the wall, and return.

He could not understand for a long time, and suddenly he realised. He started laughing and laughing.

He then let me in on the cause of his laughter, he said 'When the phone rings I have to run to the back of the house to answer it because although there's enough signal to ring the phone, if I answer it without going to the rear of the house, facing a particular wall, I will get cut off'

After the rest of the consultation he got up and thanked me. I thanked him and I said; 'It just proves it to you that we are watched by spirit, good luck, and goodbye'

* * *

Cambridge;
Eyes wide and a shocked expression...

A young lady sat down before me, she was of slight build and timid to match. As I was looking into her future a young man appeared to me, he was saying that nobody could do anything for him, and for me to tell her that she shouldn't let anybody feel bad, as there was nothing that anybody could have done, and that it was an eventuality due to the life he led.

I described to her what I was being told, and that he was only about 30 years young, on drugs, and that he took a massive overdose. I also said that he shows himself as about 5'2" and of a stocky build.

'Yes' she said 'I know who he is' with tears forming.

I said 'well he is here,'

'Oh really' she said with eyes-wide and a shocked expression.

I carried on by saying that 'he often watches you help your boyfriend that lives in an eighteenth century house the one that you both are currently emptying stuff out so that you both can decorate it.

'Yes, that's right' she replied even more surprised.

I carried on doing her future.

* * *

Esher Fair;
A Medium pipe dream.....

A nice polite woman took the hot seat, hesitantly. As she shuffled the cards I started smelling smoke, one minute it was cigarettes and the next it was a pipe tobacco. Being at outdoor events many smells waft past so I just carried on with her future.

That is until a man appeared beside this lady, he just stood there. He looked quite funny as he had a cigarette in one side of his mouth and then a pipe in the other, as this was a little strange I put up with it for a while questioning it all and thinking that I've got it wrong, I must be working too hard and need a rest. Sometimes I won't say things at first if I doubt what I am seeing, until they (head-office) persist. Then I will 'say what I see' they know how I work; so it suits all.

I thought that it was now time to get brave, 'did your father have dark hair?'

'Yes' she said

'Did he smoke cigarettes?' I asked

And again she said 'Yes'

'Did he then change to a pipe?'

'Yes' she said with a wry smile just creeping in on the edges of her mouth.

I told her that I thought I was going mad, as I keep seeing him standing there with a cigarette and a pipe, and he keeps swapping from pipe to cigarette and back again. At this point she was still smiling, she then said 'that her father had given up the cigarettes but ended up with a pipe, but then went back to the cigarettes, and that it was like this for the rest of his life'

I then informed her 'that he has been watching all of the mistakes you have been making and that he will try to guide you, if you will listen'

We pressed on with her 3 months future, and it was after that she told me that she was a medium herself and that's why I had told her during her consultation that she walks with spirit.

She stood up and looked down at me, and said, 'you are indeed a star' and shook my hand. This usually brings a tear to my eye; I wish her well with her healing work.

* * *

Somerset;
Mother knows best.......

As a consultation was coming to a close, and we were finalising details of a lady's immediate future, I knew she did not believe me. But as I handed her the tape of her reading I was suddenly compelled to say;

'Roses grow best with horse shit!! Your mother says'

Her face lit up like a lamp in a darkened cavern, she said 'I believe everything you have now said as my mother was always saying that; thank you'

* * *

Somerset;

For he has all of the answers....

A gentleman sat as I was doing his future, part of which was that I could see his bed and all of these funny dreams on a pillow, I tried to ignore it because nothing was clear at all. So I just carried on regardless.

His guide said to me, 'Ask him why he is here, as he already knows his immediate future. He thinks about it in bed, he asks us to tell him whilst he is asleep'

It's a bit bizarre, but I gave it to him straight. And when I did his face was so funny, so shocked that somebody else knew.

He stammered 'that's right, that's right'

I wish I had a camera sometimes, as their faces are so funny.

* * *

Ealing;

Three in a bed, and the Granny said.....

A very down to earth young lady sat perched aloft one of my chairs, she was about 30 years old with a pony tail, married with children.

During her reading I was transported to a furniture shop. I said to the woman, 'you have recently been shopping for furniture, haven't you?'

She nodded, a little surprised.

But that was minor to what was coming next; 'you preferred the four poster bed didn't you?' Again she nodded but was much more attentive now. 'What you didn't know about your shopping trip is that you had an extra member to your number; your grandmother.

And she's says that she was in it; testing it out for you.

As you walked past the bed she said to you 'that this is a good one' and 'I could sleep on this' 'but you just didn't hear her, did you? I said.

She was sort of smiling in disbelief, but could not discard the evidence.

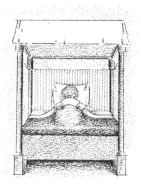

After a few more points the consultation drew its end and she left with more thoughts than when she arrived.

I like it like this way, snappy. Yes the Granny did have short curly grey hair, doesn't all grannies? But they don't all test out the beds for you in a shop; do they? Anyway, she did buy the bed.

* * *

Ealing;
Run rabbit, run rabbit, run, run, run...

I was aware of a man stood beside a nice lady who was sat shuffling the cards. He just seems grey so I left him there for a minute and just carried on with her reading, after a few minutes I said 'there is a man standing next to you, a bit stooped over, grey clothes and a grey face with grey hair. I am sorry he won't go. I have asked for a bit more but he finds it very difficult to communicate.

After a few minutes of standing next to her, he broke out into song,

Run rabbit - run rabbit - Run! Run! Run!

Bang! Bang! Bang! Bang!
Goes the farmer's gun.
So Run rabbit - run rabbit - Run! Run! Run!

I said to her that 'he was a farmer in the war and that he is now showing me his gun, it's a very long thin thing'

She said with her eyes wide open, 'how stupid of me, it's my grandfather, he was a farmer all of his life, how did I not realise this'

I said that it's because your brain goes numb when you sit there. That's all.

* * *

Ealing;
The melting Ice Maiden...

A young lady with short dark hair and fairly well spoken came for a consultation, she seemed a bit harsh but that's okay, as I get that quite a bit. A little frosty, a little nervous.

Whilst I was laying out her cards on the table, visions of a funeral procession were taking place before my eyes, there were black funeral cars and I was at the graveside watching people laying their floral tributes upon the grave. I was with the lady whose funeral it was, I explained to the young lady what I was seeing with regards to the funeral of her grandmother, and that her grandmother was making a point that the family put their flowers on the grave, but the young lady insisted upon her own floral tribute.

'Yes' she said, breaking into a little smile and a tear down one cheek. And as she did, the harshness that was evident earlier started to melt and disappear.

I said 'your Grandmother had a flat on the Isle of Wight which she left to you?' 'Yes, that's correct' the lady replied smiling, I said 'she's telling me that she knew how much you loved her, and that you were both very good friends, so much so that you told each other things that you would not tell anybody else, and she wants me to tell you that she has not left you; and she never will'

With that I gave a very choked up lady her tape and my card.

* * *

Ealing;
Teachers always want the last word......

A young man about 26 years old, said oh! Is it my turn? Whilst rubbing his hands with glee and sort of hopping from his left to right foot. He made me laugh, he was so jolly.

As I was looking at his cards a gentleman appeared. I described him in full, including a goatee black beard, with that the young man remarked, 'That sounds very much like my old science teacher'

'Well he is obviously dead now! He says that he just wanted to pop in and prove life after death' the young man laughed so loud and virtually proclaimed 'he always did want to prove he was right, and to have the last word'

As we moved on to his future I said to him 'you often smell cigarette smoke don't you?

'Yes' he said 'but I don't understand why?'

'Well' I replied 'I have a man stood beside you now, he is showing me his lips and that they were all yellow. He used to smoke roll-ups right down to the bitter end, so much so that he would have stuck a pin in if he could but the pin would have become hot as he smoked them so low. His fingers smelt of nicotine and so did he and his fingers were all yellow, and he got cancer of the tongue and throat. And that he was pleased that you don't smoke'

I looked up at this young man sat there, and he was just staring at me and he was now quiet. So much so, he was struck dumb. As this man was his favourite uncle.

I smiled at him and said 'now, when you smell the smoke you will know who it is, and you can say hello. Can't you?

He just sat there speechless, possibly for once in his life.

I finished his future and gave him his tape, he left quite enlightened and comforted. I hope he still smells him.

* * *

Ealing;
A caring person and their money are unfortunately parted easily.......

A lady with smart dark hair sat down, she was very 'prim and proper' as I laid out her cards I said to her 'I can see there was man in your life that you had got rid of, as he made you very unhappy' 'Yes' she replied.

I also said that 'there is a small child which is the sunshine of your life and no matter what life throws at you; you feel that having this child is some sort of compensation. But alas there is so much sadness in you and I feel that money has gone from you and also a friend'

I went on to saying to the lady that 'You have a very precise job and you are living under conditions that you don't wish to, and you can't see a way out. Your guide is telling me that they have heard your prayers at night but it will all take time. Until then take the love of your little girl and the love of your work'

She then decided to speak with me, she told me that she had lent money to a friend, I asked 'how much' she replied '£46,000 and he has disappeared'

She informed me that she works as a scientist, she tried to tell me about her work but it went over my head. Her husband had left her for another woman, and she hated where she is living.

Ahh, what a horrible time for her, I hope that next time I see her that things would have got better, I'm not surprised that her guide is very close to her.

* * *

Earl's Court;
Jumping Jack Flash....

A rather posh woman sat there at my table in the middle of the street at Earl's Court, I was at a charity event and the road was shut off, so we were allowed to sit in the street.

As her reading progressed I found myself in her home, I was describing her dining room to her and suddenly all I could see was a little Jack Russell dog, he was jumping up and down just to the side of my table, he wasn't interfering in any way he was just jumping up and down with all his might, with all four legs clearing the floor and nearly the top of the table every time. It was as if he were on springs. Up and down, up and down he went continuously.

He was saying 'don't forget me, don't forget me'

You know people are funny, I done her future, I visited her home and I even told her what was in her life right now! But alas not much reaction, until I saw the jumping dog and told her about it. It was only then that a reaction came by way of the beam on her face, but this said it all.

The dog's thoughts and love was still there and still very much with her and this is what she needed, and as ever, it was her little friend that knew.

* * *

Camden;

Language problems? Not a problem, when you're dead.

A girl approached me and asked in 'Broken English' 'can I have a reading please?' I nodded and beckoned her to sit down. As I started to talk to her in my regional London accent this being Cockney, She just looked at me quite confused, it was then that I realised that her command of the English lexicon was not to the level of the usual 'Tourist English' that I had grown accustomed to in metropolitan Camden.

We just sat there for a few seconds that certainly felt like minutes. We just looked at each other and then laughed whilst shrugging our shoulders. I then in 'Broken English' tried to converse with her, as I knew we had a problem, and if we couldn't really understand each other this exercise would in fact, be pointless.

Between the lines I gathered from her that she was from Poland and that we could carry on as her friend who is living with her can speak excellent English and that her friend will translate it later that day. I wasn't really happy about this but not only did I know that she wanted a reading, I also knew that she needed a reading.

As I started shuffling the cards, her mother appeared as if ordered, like Aladdin's genie from the lamp. Her mother informed me that she had died approximately one year past with stomach cancer. Of which I passed on to the best of my ability.

You will find throughout my work that there is no language barrier between Spirit and myself, whether it is a man from India or a lady from Botswana we can always communicate, the only fly in the ointment can be the sitter/client in this world.

Her mother then told me to say that she watches her daughter get on the 159 bus. Again I passed this on she smiled and said 'yes I do and it also stops outside my door' I returned the smile and carried on with her consultation till the end; she got up, thanked me and left.

I feel that we did sort of understand each other but I'm very pleased that she has somebody at home that will understand and that can explain fully in two of the languages from this world.

All of this reminds me of the body I found in France a couple of year ago. I was on holiday in Marseille with my two sons and a French friend that we knew from London; Anthony was driving as I can't drive on the right. I said to Anthony 'could you pull over please so I could spend a penny' as the car stopped I could see under the bushes what I thought was a man lying face down, with his head on his arm as if asleep. From the car which was about 15 meters from the man I said 'he's dead'

I got out and walked over to him and in my 'Broken French' I said 'pardon, pardon' but to no avail, he didn't stir. I was so sure that he was dead I put my hand down the back of his shirt, his back was stone cold, 'Oh' I said to him, 'you poor love, god bless you' As he died alone he may have been a little afraid. My friend said that she had better deal with the police as she lives in Marseille, so she called them and said that she found him, just in case there was complications or an investigation, and the last thing we needed was to travel back to France for a coroner's inquest.

Over next few days I kept giving him some distant healing whilst thinking of him, and how he died, he was about 76 years old and a possible loner, because near the scene where I found him, there was I little van that he may have lived in.

On the third day since the unfortunate find he appeared to me and said with perfect English, 'thank you'

As with all communication of this type it is telepathy with which they communicate. So no language barriers exist.

* * *

Regent's Park;
An unexpected lesson...in her thirst for knowledge...

A woman perched before me; she was very uptight but much anger deep inside more than anything else. I asked her to pick her cards, I could feel all of this anger and tremendous disappointment, but why?

Looking into the cards she had this thirst for education and I could see a child involved in this and spirit told me that she really resented this child, almost to hatred sometimes, because she had to give up her education so that she could have this little girl. I thought god, how am I going to approach this.

I cannot be any other way except honest and straight forward, so I said you have been given a beautiful little soul, but there are times when you wish that she was just simply not here, and you could go on with your educational pathway. I did expect her to be angry but all she did was nod in agreement.

I must admit as I was surprised because my whole life has been dedicated to bringing up my children.

The reading progressed through towards her future, and at the end of it I said 'could you please look at this a different way?' this little girl will grow up and if you study at home when she is a big girl you can then further your career and become a professor in your field, her face lit up.

She had been so wrapped up in regret she could not see what the future could hold for her. So I now know that she will love this tiny baby instead of resenting it. And the lady's future wasn't bad either.

It's funny what spirit makes you do to help people by they know better than I what is needed.

* * *

Regent's Park;
A little ray of light in the darkness….

A good looking, manly faced young chap sat before me, he had a lovely pair of thighs and nice eyes. I started to shuffle the cards and unexpectedly everything went instantly black and both he and myself were at the bottom of a empty water well, as I looked up through the pitch darkness there was a glimmer of light at the top, I thought to myself 'what on earth am I doing here?' there was just enough light falling to this depth, for me to make out the rough circular brick wall of the well. I touched the bricks I was suddenly back in Regent's Park during the middle of a warm sunny day in August, and I was reading for this young manly faced good looking chap. But now I was exhausted.

I looked up at him and said 'you've been to a very dark place haven't you? And it's taken a very long time for you to come back hasn't it?'

'How do you know?' he exclaimed. I replied that 'I have just been there, to the bottom of your well, with you' whilst being shocked, puzzled and nervous all at the same time he said 'yes, yes that's what I used to call it' I then said to him that 'he always feels like he is sat on the edge of this well and that he could always fall in it again'

He looked down to his hands as if ashamed and just nodded; very thoughtfully and reminiscent.

I tried to pull him from it by relaying to him what his guide was telling me, and that was 'that she was with you throughout that time and that she will try to help you to stay out of it in the future'

This information lifted him instantly, as it gave him reassurance and comfort that he wasn't on his own.

With this past we progressed on with James' future, it all looked good, rosy and much brighter than his past!

* * *

Regent's Park;
The Spirit Fairy, a fluffy dog and Alexandria.....

Everybody in my family is aware that I do not normally under any circumstances, read for children.

I came to the van to get a cup of tea; it was such a hot day. Any excuse as I'm virtually addicted to tea. It used to be coffee and cigarettes, but if the cigarettes were to go, so had the coffee.

Because for me; both walked firmly hand-in-hand.

Walking past my stall was a man and his two daughters, and in a very posh voice I heard this man say to his girls 'would you like a reading?' in a jokey and condescending fashion. One of the girls was about 15 years old and very good looking. Some might say that the younger one wasn't as attractive; she had long dark hair and was about nine years old.

The girl's father called to my lot who were manning the stall and said 'could we get the girls a reading?' the older girl then interjected very poshly, 'Oh no, I don't wish for one daddy, but thank you anyway' flashing her eyes at him, but the little one said very sincerely 'I do daddy' without speaking to anybody I unprecedented reached over and took her hand, grabbed a tape and told the father and her older sister to return in about half an hour.

All my lot on the stall stood there with mouths open, even I was amazed at what I was doing.

When I am led by spirit I never question, I just obey. And it is always right.

I knew that her father thought that I was just a bit of fun, like the ones you will find at the fairground. He never asked a price. The little girl appeared to be very content in my company. She said her name was Alexandria. I told her 'that everything I am going to do and say is very real and everything you say to me stays with me, do you understand?' 'Yes' she said nodding head quickly.

I shuffled the cards for her as her hands were too tiny; I laid the cards across the table so that she may pick them. Whilst she was choosing I looked over towards my stall and my lot still had open mouths, still shocked that I was reading for a child, even at this point, I still didn't know why I was doing this. But I was nonetheless.

It was quite funny really as there was this little girl speaking so awfully, awfully posh, and then there's me with my cockney accent.

Immediately after Alexandria had finished picking her cards and laying them on the table I was in her bedroom, I described to her a big fluffy toy dog that she talks to and said 'you tell him all of your secrets, don't you?'

'Yes' she said with her lovely blue eyes looking at me.

I then said quietly 'your doggy knows that you eat your dinners and then get rid of them in the toilet. Is that true?

Very worriedly she looked around and replied 'Yes, but don't tell daddy'

I moved on by saying 'there is a lot of pink in your bedroom, pink curtains, bedspread and as many pink clothes that you can get your hands on' 'that's right' she said. I also said to her 'last winter you got quite ill with some sort of flu and you liked the attention you got, didn't you? And you feel that your big sister takes all of the attention away from you most of the time don't you? She then put her eyes down; I said 'please don't be ashamed of anything, we all go through funny stages and sometimes we get it a bit wrong'

'Do you find that this 'not eating habit' you've got into is now out of control? And that it's not you don't want to eat; it's that you find that you just can't and that you have trained your mind to throw it up, and because of it you have lost a lot of weight already haven't you?

'Yes, 2 stone' she replied.

'Well then, let's get some good attention' I jovially said.

I continued by saying 'you will see your 'spirit fairy' (*This is how her guide asked me to put it so that she would be able to accept it*) in your bedroom, and I want you to draw her for me and send the picture to me. I know what she looks like and I will tell you if you got it right'

(*I didn't say this to Alexandria, but she will appear with wings, a wand and blue glitter all over*)

Your spirit fairy says that 'you will get extra attention by eating extra helpings, bit by bit little by little, and that will create joyful attention which is good. Your spirit fairy also says 'that you have a lovely singing voice and if you use that talent you will get more attention'

I then said to her 'I am going to give you my home telephone number you can phone me whenever you wish to talk, and you know that you can tell me anything you wish to. I also will give you a meditation cd and I would like you to do it every day with my compliments. I am only at the other end of the telephone, with that she then came over to my chair spontaneously to cuddle me; it was like cuddling a bag of bone.

I thought that I must speak to her father when he and the older sister came back. When they did return I waved Alexandria's tape in front of her old sister and said 'you will not touch this nor will you touch her cd' I also said to the father 'please encourage Alexandria to telephone me' he then said 'how much is that?' 'Nothing' I said, 'no charge'

I proceeded to tell the father, 'I do know that you don't realise that what I do is very real and it is important you encourage her to listen to her cd. Please let her telephone me'

My heart goes out to this little girl and I sincerely hope that she makes it, she had set a bad wheel in motion that was out of control, and I certainly hope her guide pulled it back. God bless her.

Somerset;
The Potato men….

A middle aged lady sat before me and all I could see was a potato. 'Oh god I thought here we go………… I'm saying nothing for a while about what I could see'

I carried on with her reading and we moved on to her future.

A lady from spirit suddenly jumped in and blurted out 'she keeps knocking on lots of doors, estate agents doors and solicitor's doors trying to find land in Scotland to build a house. I've been with her! Tell her I've been with her'

I was taken aback slightly by the voraciousness of this lady from spirit. I gathered myself and said to the sitter 'There is a lady with us and she says that you have been looking for land in Scotland, she says that you have been knocking on many doors to find this land for sale. And she has repeatedly told me to tell you that she has been with you in Scotland; knocking on those doors'

The middle aged lady in front of me was just sat there, stunned like a rabbit caught in the headlights of on oncoming vehicle; trying to understand it all.

'Yes. I ...... I have been in Scotland, and knocking on doors trying to buy some land, as I want to build a house' she replied

'But how do you know this?' asked the lady?

Just then the spirit lady once again jumped in and instructed me to say about the potato, 'tell her it isn't cooked!'

I imparted this to her but to no avail.

I carried on by saying 'the lady also informs me that she comes from your old school and it was she that used to look after the children on rainy days when they couldn't go out to play, and she would make potato men and get you kids to do it'

'Oh my god, Oh, No' she gasped with her hand over her mouth.

I thought thank god for that, I'm not going mad. At least were found out why the potato was here.

'It's my old teacher. Well, teaching assistant. She was the helper at the school. We used to put matchsticks in the potatoes for arms and legs. Mind you they never stood up they just sort of rolled around on their backs like an upside-down turtle. We would paint them too, faces and clothes; it was such fun' she said, whilst smiling, reminiscing of days long gone.

I said to her 'that this lady says that she will still be knocking on doors with you, trying to guide you in the right direction'

As the reading drew to a close she got up, thanked me; and left.

* * *

Somerset;

Being undemanding, is it hereditary?

A man in his fifties took the preverbal hot seat; I unexpectedly saw him in his bath, and no ladies I didn't look down.

He found the bath a place to ponder all of his questions and answers in there, a place of peace and quiet; a place to let his mind run free.

I said to him 'you have sometimes wondered if the tall shadow you see is real or imaginary, well I am to tell you that it's your father and he is here now. He is stood here next to you, and his clothes are all grey. He doesn't want to say anything particular he just wants to stand next to you in case I say something that isn't quite right, just to ensure that I get your future correct; but if I do go astray he will interject.

When I had finished the man in his fifties wandered off and so did his father. What had struck me throughout the consultation was that both he and his father were so undemanding.

* * *

Bristol;

The Black Car will come for him soon.

A nice chubby down to earth person sat before me, she was a little hesitant and excited all at the same time.

We continued towards the 'future' section of her consultation when suddenly I was shown a man in the garden of a bungalow; he then walked off into the house, but he swiftly returned with chair in hand, he walked to the front of the garden and promptly sat upon the chair next to the short garden gate. He just sat there by the gate, staring across the road at the lady sat before me.

So I described what I was seeing to her, and I then sat as he would and pulled his face for her, 'yes' she said 'that's him, the nasty one' I said to her, 'yes he is a very nasty man, and he really hates you doesn't he?'

'Yes, that face you pulled looks just like him' she retorted.

I then chuckled and said 'Well, your dad is here and he's telling me all of this, and although you are smiling to cover it up, it really upsets you terribly, doesn't it?' She nodded in agreement.

'He is also telling me that a black car will come for him soon, and the problem will be gone, and the whole street will be pleased as he hates everybody, not just you. So don't feel singled out.'

We then progressed with her future which was quite good. Her dad popped back as he had decided to put on a very light blue tie. With that she cried as it was the last thing she bought for him. Well he is showing it off at the moment, he is telling me about a man called Mick who is a business man. And I also keep hearing a song by Ian Dury which is Drugs and Sex and Rock And Roll. Just don't get involved with his business or you could get involved with things you don't want to.

At least she left warned and on guard.

* * *

Bristol;

No escape from 'The Boys in Blue'

A woman shuffled her cards, she then spread them out choosing a few, and during her future cards I kept seeing the police.

I said 'are you in trouble with the police?'

'No' she said, she then kept saying 'I have had nothing to do with the police, never had'

So I kept on with her reading but again I saw the police, but this time it was a police car just travelling up and down the road. I relayed this to her and she kept saying 'no'

So spirit then showed me the vision again but now they put a blue light on it and sent it up and down the road again, only this

time flashing. I put this to her and again the answer was 'no'
So once again we carried on with her future reading.

Again, another vision came but this time all the 'boys in blue' were standing by this car. I asked again 'nothing to do with police?' 'No' she said.

I was really fed up now; I said to her 'how long have you had your new car for?' 'Not long' she replied, 'we bought it at the auction, the police put their old cars in them.'

Well you can imagine my face; I just looked at her, 'so you have got a police car' 'yes' she said, hanging her head in shame.

'Well' I said, 'get rid of it, as it's going to let you down' and I laughed at the fact how spirit guides are always right.

* * *

Bristol;
She's a bit of an old Croc...

A young lady of 25 years or thereabouts sat and shuffled the cards. As she was doing so an old lady arrived, I thought 'Oh no I'm going to ignore her for a while. How can you say to a young person that I have a little old lady here from the world of spirit with grey short hair, a coat and a handbag?

No I thought, so I said to the old lady I'm sorry but you will have to just stand there until you find something positive that this young girl can manage to recognise, in the mean time I shall carry on with her present and future reading. With this the old lady kept wiggling this handbag at me from one side to the other, and she insisted that I should have a really, really good look at it. She was very insistent.

The bag was a bit large, brown in colour and made from crocodile skin, she just stood there and kept moving this handbag from side to side, I thought that maybe this is important, so I struck and said to the young girl 'do you know why this little old lady that's standing next to me is showing me a rather large brown crocodile skin handbag?'

(You always know when you have hit on the right note as their faces light up before they speak.)

She looked up and said 'that's my old babysitter; the old lady loved that bag. She left it to me and I've got it wrapped up in tissue paper in a box at home'

'Well' I said with a laugh 'she has borrowed it to prove something to you that she is here. She is also saying 'don't be sad as a young man will be here soon'

So she left taking her old lady, the Croc bag and the hope of a young man with her.

* * *

Cambridge;
A stony past...

A somewhat butch lady sat down for a consultation. During the reading I could feel a spirit but couldn't see it, I just seemed to know that 'she, the lady from spirit, lived by a stony seaside area'

I said to the lady what I knew but she was unable to place it. So with such little information I continued her future as more info often comes later.

'I loved to grow roses' the lady shouted, and I then saw her riding a bike. So once again I explained what I was hearing and seeing; but still the answer was a resounding 'No'

So I went back to her future cards, during which I kept hearing the sea crashing on stones. I again asked this lady 'are you sure that you don't know of this spirit woman who lived by the sea' and she answered 'No'

So I just kept on with a straight reading trying to shut the spirit woman out. As I finished with this rather butch lady, the spirit woman shouted out 'I don't like tea, I never drink the horrible stuff'

I told the lady this, and as if she was blasted by a bolt from the heavens she said 'yes, yes, it's my dad's auntie'

And I then asked 'did she live at a seaside that was stony?'

'Well, not really' was her reply.

'Where did she live then?' I asked

'Oh Goring, in the county of Sussex' I could not believe my ears, as Goring is on the sea, hence the name Goring-By-the-Sea. I know the area quite well, and it is stony with that the spirit woman left.

So we wrapped up the reading and the butch lady left.

* * *

Cambridge;
Sisters are doing for themselves.....

A very Butch Lesbian came into the van due to the rain pouring with force from the heavens. As she came in I must admit I was a bit perturbed as I don't book them in; my son does. So I sometimes feel a bit threatened when I cannot see who is coming into my van, in case I can't get them out again but saying that I have never had a problem before.

But the whole van thing stinks of 'Gypsy-Rose-Lee' I am sure that there could be a few real clairvoyants amongst the 'Gypsy-Rose-Lee's of this world, but I have always liked to keep it outside of the van where everybody can see me and I can see them.

So we proceeded with the consultation, I quickly found myself deposited in a room which was green, and I mean green everything! Walls, curtains, settee and chairs; just green everywhere.

I said to her 'I have your mother here. Did she like green?'

'Yes' she said, nodding whilst starting to cry.

I went on to say that 'she's telling me that you both got on very well, and that you could talk to her about anything, as she did not have a problem with your way of life. In fact she tells me that she was slightly the same way'

And me being cheeky I said 'it's lucky she didn't go the whole way or you wouldn't be here'

Wiping her tears away, I suddenly saw her sister. I then said to her 'that if your mother had been a fully practicing lesbian you would not have had the pleasure of a sister who is also here from the world of spirit. She doesn't look like you though; she is much taller and thinner, isn't she?' 'Yes' she said blowing her nose.

I said that they are both telling me that you must stop worrying about your job, it will be fine. She was so relived, I said 'well...let's do your future for the next three months' it turned out that she worked in the T.V industry. By me slightly prejudging her I was proved very wrong; she was a very nice and caring person.

* * *

Greenford;
Just keeps talking.....

A tall woman wearing a brown jumper with pearls strewn around her neck was shuffling the cards; she looked very attractive in her outfit. In her cards I could see this very tall building; it was like a block of flats or offices and to get to the top a lift is needed. I told her that 'when you get to the top there is all this talking you have to do, but you give over money in order for you to do this talking'

She nodded in agreement.

'I am also to tell you that it is doing you no good at all, everybody thinks that you are ok on the face of it, yet you feel that you are sliding down and nobody can see it; can they?' 'And you need a different way rather than going over and over things as it is not helping. You must laugh and try to lift yourself up' She was very quiet up to this point, she then told me 'she has to go to the top of this building once a week as she was have psychotherapy and she even thought that it wasn't doing her any good whatsoever'

The funny thing is that she told me is that she is a psychotherapist herself. I told her 'perhaps some spirit healing with no talking at all would be better'

I gave her one of my meditation cd's. Complimentary of course; much to my son Anthony's continued annoyance, but I am in this person's heart and money does not matter.

I did her future and I hope she stopped talking about miserable stuff, and that my cd would lift her up, I certainly know that her guide is with her, and as I told her 'she can talk to him all she likes'

* * *

Kent;
A butcher, a Baker and a French Waiter?

Whilst I was going through a woman's cards with her, I suddenly saw a white apron, it was on a man. It was not an older man; I knew this as he had no tummy. I said what I was seeing to the woman; she asked 'is it a butcher?' So I looked at the white apron again and I said 'no, as there's no blood, it's a clean apron'

The then picture changed and he showed me his face, he had dark hair with a moustache and he was about 35-40 years of age. And he was standing beside a cream coloured van which had red lettering down the side. I couldn't make out what it said. I could tell that this van came from the 50's or 60'.

I said to the woman 'that I thought by the apron that he was a French waiter by the way it was worn' 'No' she said, 'it's my brother! He was a baker' 'Oh I replied, I've never had a baker and a van before'

When I had finished her cards and gave her tape to her, I said 'you don't seem happy; there is something you wanted but did not get from this consultation?' 'Yes' she said 'you're right, I didn't want my brother; I wanted my son. Nobody has ever given my son to me'

I very gently told her, 'it is hard for you to understand but because you want him so much, it stops him coming due to the intensity of the love and emotion you have for him'

For comfort I said 'next time we meet we will have to try something that is hard but can be accomplished, and that is to give you some healing before we start doing your reading so that we can just send gentle love and not high emotion or a negative energy field which is created by the desperation of hearing from your son. Being a mother myself I don't know what you feel like and I would not insult you by saying that even if I try to imagine what you feel like I would just get upset'

But at least her future was bright and cheerful, and may her god be with her and help her.

* * *

Camden;
Brian? That's a funny name for an Angel.

A nice girl found me at the back of the market, she said 'I never come to this part, and I don't know why I came in here until I saw you' I laughed! I said to her 'that a lot of people say a similar thing, as if they were just pushed down here'

She sat down, and as I was doing her cards I saw her in her kitchen, dancing. I said this to her and she found that fascinating.

I then said 'there seems to be a young man that watches you. But you don't see him in the kitchen. You have a garden don't you?' She nodded.

'And in that garden you have a bench; it's on a big slab of concrete isn't it?' Again she nodded.

I carried on by saying 'You seem a bit young to me to have bought your house, and it's more like the countryside than around here. I feel that it's around the Cambridge area?' 'Yes' she said somewhat shocked that I could know so much about where she lived considering that it's nearly 100 miles away.

'There's a young man here with us' I said 'he's about 6'3" tall with a nice figure and a nice kind face, and he says that that you see him in the garden by the bench, is that true? A little nod again confirmed that it was.

I then had to pluck up the courage to say to her what was coming next, as he was telling me to describe him,

'IN FULL! And don't leave anything out!!'

He was very insistent of that.

Well here goes I thought; I leant forward and said to the girl, 'this may come as a bit of a surprise to you, as it certainly has for me, but this young man has asked me to describe him in full to you and that he is very insistent that I shouldn't leave anything out'

She looked very inquisitively at me. I then proceeded; 'this young man looks, like an angel, he has no clothes on and luckily I can only see the top half of him. He also has beautiful cream wings'

To my astonishment she did not run from me, 'shouting mad woman, mad woman lock her up' instead she smiled and said;

'His name is Brian, and he's my friend'

I asked her 'is this the only way that you can accept him?'

She nodded and smiled.

I returned the smile to say that I understood, and I then said 'Brian tells me that you were all in a large group of friends together and that you all worked in the city as computer whizz-kids. And that he was in a fast car that crashed, you were not lovers but very good friends and the only way you know that seeing spirit is not a bad thing, is if you see wings'

Well, she said as the reading came to its inevitable close, 'I am glad I walked down here, god bless you Collette'

She kissed me on my cheek and left, leaving me with a little tear in my eye. Ahhhhh.

* * *

Watford;
Her Blood Red Dress.

My cousin Marion has a pub in Apsley which is just outside Watford in Hertfordshire. She calls me in to have a 'consultation evening' sometimes. On one occasion I was called in, not for an evening just as a favour, as a very close friend to her was in trouble and needed some advice. So upon a train I hopped to go out there. I do like train journeys.

Marion my cousin made me some tea, and showed me to my chair. She then beckoned the lady over to sit also.

I looked at the lady and said 'please don't speak to me, just say yes, or no' this because many people just sit down and start blabbing which makes my job harder if the same information comes up in the reading the sitter thinks that I'm just using the information gleaned from them as they were blabbing at the start.

'Just shuffle the cards' I said. As she was holding the cards I was suddenly looking at a young lady from the world of spirit who was wearing a red dress, she was holding it out, fanning it from the bottom.

The spirit girl then said 'No, not red' she then held it out again and it was full of blood, and she had to make sure that I knew that it was blood and not just the colour red.

She then took me in a car which was going round a bend, I described all of this to the lady opposite and her mouth just fell open.

I said 'the dead girl had similar hair to mine, she had an oval face and she was only about 17 years of age. And it was on the bend where she just took me that she died. The boyfriend was driving and they had both been drinking'

She then showed me books and told me that she worked in a library and her name was Jane. Wow! What a communicator I thought, if only they were all like this my job would be so easy.

As I looked up at the lady still holding the cards I could see the tears streaming down her face; this was her friend. I said 'I'm so sorry; once it starts I cannot stop it'

The lady said that her friends name was Jane, and that they were the best of friends.

I asked Jane 'what she wanted, i.e.; what was the message for this woman sat before me'

Jane said 'that she had come to give the woman strength to leave the man who Jane had watched slapping her about' I passed this on to the lady and she just sobbed some more, I don't know if it was because of her beloved friends passing or that because she now knew that there are more people that know about the abuse she has been suffering.

Her future when we got around to doing the cards was a bit rocky, but at the end of three months (as I will only read for three months) she was pulling through it all and to a brighter stronger future.

Many months later I asked my cousin how the woman was fairing, she said that she was a lot better after she left the man that she was with. I could not make any comment as client confidentially stands whoever the client or the enquirer maybe.

* * *

Scotland, Isle of Bute 3rd floor;
The mystery tinkler...

My son I and were helping a friend decorate their home on the lovely Isle of Bute in bonnie Scotland. I was very busy sweeping up and, I was going down the hallway as I wanted to go and sweep up in the bathroom, I could see a tall man through the obscure misty glass on the door. I thought that my son Anthony must be working in there so I'll go and do something else as the bathroom isn't big enough to fit us both in.

Anthony then came walking down the hallway and I said 'oh you've finished in the bathroom?' he replied 'I haven't been in the bathroom I've been in the bedroom'

So the question remains, who was in the bathroom???

* * *

Scotland, Isle of Bute, 2nd floor;
We met upon the stairs.

Whilst returning from taking some rubbish from my friend's home down the stairs to the bins, I was met by a spirit lady. She was wearing clothes from about 1901; these were a full length black skirt with a white high necked blouse with 'leg of mutton' sleeves. A brooch at the throat and she was atopped with a largish hat, she was about 30 years of age.

As I was going up the stairs she sort of blocked

my pathway as she was descending and I ascending, and as soon as I saw her and without hesitation or thought I said to her 'not today I'm not working'

I often think about her, and wonder what she wanted.

* * *

Scotland, Edinburgh;
The Haunted B&B.........

On a trip to Edinburgh with my youngest son Robie, we stayed in a very strange bed & breakfast for just one night.

Upon arrival we discovered it to be an ex-tenement block which was identical to the rest of the road which was full of these terraced blocks of flats, normally in each block would be 6-8 flats.

The whole building was not what I expected at all. To get to our bedrooms we had to rise to the top of the building via the stairs, 90 of them to be precise. It was more like a summit.

But for breakfast we had to go one flight down to a different flat. After a good night sleep my son and I went down to the dining room.

We sat and we were promptly served breakfast tea (I do like my tea) I was surveying the room from my chair and on my left side was an old brick built fireplace.

I remember thinking whilst my eyes wandered around the rest of the room 'what a long way to carry the coal up to the flats, up all of those stairs' so heavy and hard back then before gas central heating.

My attention was then drawn back towards the fireplace which was on my left; this is quite funny, as nearly everything I see regarding the spirit world is on my left. In front of the fireplace kneeling before some brick shelves which grew up from the hearth, was a woman with her back to me, as if she were cleaning out the ashes from the fire. She had very long thick black hair which trailed down her cream coloured blouse towards her mauve skirt.

Without turning around she started talking to me, but it was my thoughts that she was answering, she said 'yes it was hard back then, damp and cold and if we could afford the coal we didn't mind carrying it all the way up here to keep warm. Just carrying it up here warmed us up'

She then said 'haven't they made the place nice'

I turned to Robie and said to him 'look over there it's a ghost, she used to live here'

Just then the lady kneeling by the fire chimed in and said 'used to? I still live here, and I pray here every day after I light the fire; as my religion is Wicca and this is my altar.

My son Robie suggested that we should tell the Bed & Breakfast owner, I said 'no, as it will just freak her out'

I often think of the Wicca witch, I had a feeling that we knew each other before.

* * *

Epson;
I didn't go under the Mistletoe....

I was called to a private house for a lady of about 50 earth years. She was quite good looking for her age; I should imagine she was a real looker in her younger days. She had shoulder length blonde hair and a good figure.

It was her daughter who called me in as a present for her mother.

I was in the lady's kitchen at her table, we got ourselves comfortable and we began. I suddenly looked up whilst she was shuffling the cards and a man had appeared beside the kitchen sink, he said to me,

'This is where I would cuddle my wife whilst she was washing the dishes' I told her and she acted quite funny.

That's strange; I thought she would be pleased.

I looked back over towards the husband, he then told me what the problem was, he said 'that after he died, his wife found a card; it was a Christmas card from another woman, but it wasn't that it was from another woman that disturbed her, it was the fact that he kept it for a few years. And it was this that broke her up inside'

He then asked me to sort this out with her. To tell her that he was not having an affair with this woman; so I passed this new and possibly revelationary piece information to her.

She just lifted her head, raised her eyebrows and with her tight lips she said 'Oh, really' in a very condescending manner of complete and utter contempt.

Leaving that to one side for the time being we moved onto her now and future section of her reading.

As the consultation was approaching its natural end, I said to her 'here is your tape and please don't think badly of your husband, he is still at the kitchen sink and you do feel his arms around you and you smell him, don't you?' She nodded.

I continued, 'If his love was not true he would not be hanging around you, and he is here a lot, isn't he?'

Again she nodded....... and smiled.

* * *

Ealing;
Carry your guilt, no more.

Sadly, my Golden retriever 'Honey' that was 17 years young, had cancer. After many battles we had to say goodbye.

I still see her now and then, but without warning she suddenly stands by my side. It's very nice, but if I am just passing the time of day with somebody it is very hard to keep taking as if Honey as not appeared because the other person would think you are mad, I always must remember that they can't see what I can, so I must pretend that she is not there and carry on.

Just a few days had passed after she died and I was terribly upset about it. I wondered how I would get on with my readings. My son Anthony who looks after the stall enquired 'will you be okay?'

'Well,' I said, 'I will try; it's better than sitting here at home just to mope about'

I did a few reading okay and thought I would be fine for the rest of the day until this woman sat down. As she started to shuffle the cards I felt really ill, my hands started shaking and my head spinning.

Oh no, I thought it's my nerves, they are worst than I thought. I'll give this woman a refund and cancel all of the bookings.

Suddenly I saw why, a man from spirit was standing there next to me, but so close, and so powerfully overwhelming. I instructed him to stand back, which he did. The intensity of this feeling subsided slightly but not enough. Again I asked him to retreat further; wow, that felt better.

I put my head down to read the cards again, and phew my stomach jumped with nerves, he was back at my table. I asked my guides to take him and hold him further away, after they done this I felt much better as he was now about 20ft away, and contained. He was ordered by my guides to stay put.

This poor woman sitting there in front of me had no idea of what just took place. Whilst I was doing her future and past I was also asking the man why he was here.

He told me, 'this lady in front of you is a nurse; she was my nurse when I was here on earth in my body. Whilst she was off duty I killed myself and she has blamed herself ever since'

I put this to her and she did cry, she said 'I never spotted how ill he was and I left him at the psychiatric ward. It was a bank holiday and I had a few days off, and when I came back he was dead'

I leant over the table and held her hand, and whilst pointing towards the grass with my other hand, I said, 'he's standing just over there, he wants you to feel not guilty, he says he felt so bad all of the time and life just wasn't worth going on with'

'And to be honest with you' I said 'when he came close to me earlier, I just wanted to just lie on the grass and die myself.

Nobody should feel like that, he's absolutely fine now and you must not feel guilty anymore'

Just a she was getting up I added 'he says that there is a nice surprise for you soon, by way of a romance in about one month.

* * *

Ealing;
'Give them my love'

An Australian girl sat down for a reading, as I was telling her to shuffle the cards I could hear a man's voice, he started to sing an old war song;

Pack up your troubles in your old kit bag
and smile, smile, smile.....

I know all of these songs because my dad made me sing them whether I liked them or not. The man appeared just off to my left, and just stood there; he was about 5ft away from me. He stood that far off so he could show his knobbly knees to me.

Mind you although he had knobbly knees he was nice looking

as he stood there in his cream khaki uniform with his short trousers, tunic and one side of his hat buttoned up.

He had a cigarette in his mouth which was held by his lovely white teeth, and grinning a big smile for me. He looked fairly youngish to me; he said that he was 30 years old.

I asked the young lady if she knew him 'No' she said.

Well, I'm used to that I thought, but spirit being the way they are, they always finds a way. The man then said to me 'he was a prisoner of war'

I explained to the girl what he said, and she replied 'no'

So I carried on with her cards. In the mean time he just stood there smoking and thinking of something else to say, suddenly he sparks up, 'tell her, I did not die in the war; I went home again' I done his bidding but to no avail, she still did not know who he was.

He started thinking again which was quite funny to watch because he was stood there, with his arms folded. But with one hand on the side of his face trying his best, to find what to say next.

As I carried on with her future, he said 'tell her I was the only one in the family who went to war, and there is a photo of me in my uniform, with the family'

The young lady wasn't upset, she had the biggest smile. She was so pleased 'that's my uncle' she laughingly said 'and you are so right with his description' 'Well, I can't get it wrong' I replied 'he's standing just there with a big satisfied smile'

She then said excitedly 'thank you, I can't wait to phone home and tell them'

As she left hurriedly with her tape in hand, he shouted out to her,

'Give them my love'

But she couldn't hear him and she

was too far for me to say anything.

* * *

Scotland;
An Invitation, Oooo I like a bit of fun!

One of my sons has a property in Scotland. If something goes wrong he has a telephone number for the local handyman company. Well, the shower decided to pack up and I was enlisted to telephone the handyman. His secretary by the name of Hazel answered; I have spoken to her on a number of occasions before.

She's a lovely lady but the problem with her is that she is so easy to pick up on clairvoyantly that is. She was talking to me for a while whilst I was desperately trying to hold back what I am picking up. If it gets too strong I have to give it.

I could see all of these creased clothes and all throughout the conversation it would not go away, so I had to tell her; gently. I said to her 'you have caused some trouble in a few places recently, and now you have to iron all of these things out? 'Yes' she said.

I then saw a baby floating by, but going by the sound of Hazel's voice she's possibly past it. So there must be a grandchild on its way. I asked Hazel if this were true, 'yes' she said. She then continued by saying that 'it was the cause of all those troubles which need ironing out'

I replied to Hazel that this message is from spirit, 'This is supposed to happen'

I do find these situations very difficult when I'm not supposed to be working as I then have to explain my work to a total stranger, never mind.

One week later she telephoned back, to say the shower is fixed. As soon as she spoke, I was shown an invitation, 'Oh no, not again I thought' so I said to hazel 'when you go home you will get an invitation to a wedding or a dinner and dance, or some kind of gathering of people'

I then added 'I have an older man here, he's looking in a mirror whilst fastening a neck tie, and it's yellow in colour with stripes, and he has a white shirt on. He keeps on showing me this yellow striped tie. It looks like he's getting ready for this event which the invitation is for, the one that you are going to get'

'Ooooo she said I can't' wait, a nice bit of fun'

I continued by saying 'take note though, as the yellow striped tie is very important, keep a look out for it at the gathering. The man just keeps showing me him putting it on and saying nothing, so the importance is the tie'

A few months went by, I telephoned Hazel for my son, she said 'Oh, Collette I don't think I want to talk to you, as I find you very scary' Surprised I said 'why? What's the matter?'

'What's the matter?' She retorted!!

'Last time we spoke you told me of an invitation that I was to receive. Well, I got it three days later; it was to the funeral of my father-in-law. We knew he was ill, but we didn't know he was going to die.

He wore that yellow tie and a white shirt at his funeral. It should have made sense to me earlier as he always wore that yellow striped tie.

I said to hazel, 'he must have told me whilst he was unconscious or his guide did. I am sorry for you, but I find it fascinating, just how he conversed with me during his sleep, whilst you were talking to me on the phone.

Hazel and I still speak, but because she's very guarded and afraid. I don't pick up much from her anymore; she has blocked it without realising it.

* * *

Ealing;

Sucking lemons

A dark headed woman sat before me looking very glum indeed; but so would you if you had your arm in a sling and a busted shoulder. She told me when I enquired, that it had just been operated on and she was a bit short of cash as she couldn't work so it was her husband who had to do extra hours at work to bring in the extra bucks to pay the bills. All of this made her a fed up and a bit guilty.

I shuffled the cards for her due to her incapacity. I instructed her that she was to tell me to stop shuffling when it 'felt right' whilst we were going through her now and future sections, my healing guides were all around her.

Her absolute immediate future I told her was a really happy time, and money coming in. Well her face said it all, her thoughts were; I disbelieve you, you fraud, I have wasted the money I have not got, you have disappointed me. I have just sucked lemons.

Well, I laughed and said, 'You just wait as see what happens next'

I carried on with her future and gave her, her tape which she took with a snarl.

The next day the jazz festival was packed. I am the only medium at all of the places I go to. I saw the same woman again, she just stood about 20 yards from me and shouted 'You were right, you were right' over and over again with everybody looking, she bounded over the best she could with her injured wing. Her face was radiantly glowing and her eyes dancing with excitement, she seemed so different. Her husband was with her this time. As she put some money in my Trinity Hospice collection pot which I keep on my table, she said, 'you were right about the money I certainly didn't believe you, I have just won the National Lottery!!! You were right'

No not the millions though; just enough to ease her troubled mind.

I expect she will be back next year for more 'lemon sucking'

* * *

Kew Fayre;
'I will walk the walk with you, till the end of the walk'

A very demure little old lady sort of perched before me on the chair, she had impeccable manners. Her name was Mrs West; I knew this as it was on her booking ticket. Usually on the booking tickets its first names only, but with this lady being so prim & proper I expected that at the time of booking she would have insisted upon her full title. But that is the sort of person she was. I later found this to be correct.

I asked her to shuffle the cards so we may start. But whilst she was fulfilling my request I heard a male voice talking to me, he was saying 'say lodger to her, say lodger to her'

I looked at her and thought that there's no way this prim & proper lady would have a lodger, I should imagine equally prim & proper home. So I carried on.

A man smart wearing a black suit appeared, and he was smoking. He said 'these are woodbines' flicking the ash from the end as he spoke.

'I'll mention this, but I'm not talking about a lodger' I said to him.

No way would this lady have had a lodger.

I mentioned what I was seeing and hearing whilst omitting the lodger bit, she told me 'unfortunately I cannot place such a man'

After that he stood there smoking his woodbines and thinking how to jog her memory so that she may remember him once again the way she did before.

In her present cards I found that she was physically exhausted and in a state of mental anguish with regard to the situation that both Mrs. West and her husband were in. I could see he was very sick and she was spending sleepless nights thinking how she could cope with him but at the same time try to do what was best for the both of them, but mainly for him, but also without her feeling that she's letting him down or giving up on him. The burden she carried was; should she move him into a residential care home, he has Alzheimer's disease.

The consultation progressed onto her future cards.

The man with the woodbines and a black suit came shooting back suddenly saying, 'tell her sandwiches! She made me sandwiches, and I was her lodger'

He seemed so insistent so I gave in. I must ask you Mrs West, 'the man that is with us in the black suit who has been smoking his woodbines keeps telling me he was your lodger, and you made his sandwiches'

Her face lit up, 'and I used to cook his dinner' Mrs. West replied.

So he was your lodger? I asked

'Yes' she said, 'for years'

I continued 'He's telling me you had a love for each other. A great respect for each other, not lovers though'

That's right' she said clutching her handbag and folded gloves that were laid upon her lap. Your lodger tells me that 'it is time your husband must be looked after by others. And that you have done enough, more than most in the world would do'

He also has instructed me that I must get this next message exactly correct, it is simply;

'I will walk the walk with you, till the end of the walk'

She was in tears, floods of tears.

To be honest, the love that these two people still share is so beautiful because of its purity. I had to take a break afterwards.

A wonderful job I feel I have.

I do often feel very humble.

* * *

Kew Fayre;
Fudge for Africa

Another stall holder whom I will refer to as 'the fudge lady' was itching to have a reading all day, but alas she gets no preferential treatment as everybody is pre-booked. We run a virtual queuing system, this being that we take pre-paid booking slots at events, so everybody gets a generous time slot. Therefore she had to book in. And the only space available was the end of the day; this is because at some events if I have been there the previous year there is often a six hour wait.

The fudge lady was around 60 years old, so I was very surprised with her reading. The first thing that happened was a man showing me a fence; it was white and small, like a picket fence in suburbia. I was drawn to lots of flowers in a private garden.

The man carried on by saying 'tell her it's in Kent, it's my garden and it's in Kent' he then threw a name at me, 'Fred'

I relayed to her what I was being told.

She sat very quiet; she then chimed in and said 'that's my dad'

I didn't really know which way to tell her the rest, so I just did;

'He tells me that you're not happy with your husband, and you want to leave him'

'Yes' she said 'I've had enough of him'

I enquired to the fudge lady, 'I think I met him this morning, he's the one with the trailer isn't he? I thought he was okay'

'No' she retorted 'he maybe to you, but he's certainly not to me'

Ahhh that's a shame I thought.

I continued 'Your father is showing me to a patch of land and it's in a very hot country. I'm looking down on tin roofs and he's telling me that you give money to these people who are very poor'

She just nodded, in agreement.

'Gosh' I said 'I feel I'm in Africa, and it's there that you send money?'

Just then it all came together, I looked at her and said 'you wish to leave your husband so that you can go and live there, and it is on this plot of land that you want to build your house, isn't it?' she still just nodded.

Well I would never have guessed by just looking at these two. I carried on by saying 'and it's your sister who will go with you' the fudge lady just sat there very quietly throughout this whole reading.

Suddenly she said 'it's all true, I've been going out there for years and I've got a nice piece of land there'

'Well' I replied 'I don't think that it's imminent, not this year anyway.

As the consultation progressed from the now to the future I said, 'let's look into your future for the next couple of months shall we?'

* * *

Kingston;

A confessional with no judgement

A middle aged woman sat looking into her own cards, I could see she was nobody's fool; I felt one first instance that she was very kind, she was fairly trim, with auburn hair.

I kept seeing her listening to people, I could also see that she did not trust me at first, but slowly she could see I was for real.

To my left I could see a noose; it was just swinging by the lady's shoulder. It was made from fairly thin rope, it was maroon in colour. I just left it hanging there for a while, and said nothing about it yet.

As we were moving through her future cards the rope changed to being big, thick and grey. It then quickly reverted back to being maroon and thin. Most odd I thought, I asked spirit what all of this was about, and very quickly they put in my mind that this thin rope is for a woman, and this thick grey one will be for a man. So therefore from now on when I see either of the ropes in a consultation it will be symbolic of a hanging, of either a man or woman.

Just to clarify this I asked spirit 'if the message that I am getting is correct, i.e. a thick one for a man and a thin one for a woman' I then requested that they so show me again, but this time to leave the rope I am to speak about.

They showed me the big grey one, just flashed it, and took it away. So at this lady's shoulder was left a thin slim rope, maroon in colour, and it just stayed there.

All of this happened in a few seconds so the lady sat opposite had no knowledge of what preceded our conversation.

I felt I needed to get back to what I saw earlier regarding her listening to people. I started by saying 'I feel that you listen to people once a week, and I would say it's very tiring almost like being in a confessional with no judgement'

I told her what I had been seeing and hearing regarding the ropes, she looked at me a bit weird as if I were a little on the odd side, but she didn't comment.

I enquired 'Do you know a woman who hanged herself?'

She looked at me in disbelief.

'Please don't speak' I quickly said 'just nod yes or no' as she looked like she was ready to burst and that's not helpful to me.

I relayed to her that this lady who hanged herself says 'she was your friend but you couldn't help her, nobody could that night. So please don't feel guilty anymore; it wasn't yours or anybody else's fault'

She tells me, 'that's why you do this listening, and you are helping people and you often question if you are really helping them'

'I do, I do' she blubs through a hanky.

Your friend says; 'The answer is yes'

The lady smiles whilst tears still

stream down her face.

'But what is this listening you do I asked?'

'I am in the Samaritans' I joined after my friend committed suicide so that I could possibly help others in similar situations.

Just then her friend jumped in, I told her that her friend says 'she helps you in your work and that you are both making a difference, together'

I handed her the tape which had her consultation on and said, 'it is so nice to see people doing good in the world'

Goodbye.

* * *

S.A.G.B HQ, Belgrave square;
Spirit are wonderful

Whilst working at Belgrave Sq, in London which is the Spiritualist Association Headquarters of Great Britain. I was asked to do a party for 6 people in Chelsea. So we arranged a time and date for the gathering to happen.

Unfortunately the day before I was due to arrive I fell badly whilst walking along a remote tow-path somewhere nr Paddington Station accompanied by my youngest son, Robie.

I couldn't walk even one pace, I can normally deal with pain but this was unbelievable and unbearable. But me being me I carried on trying to walk against my son's wishes, after a couple of more paces my son said that he wouldn't aid me to walk anymore as I may be doing myself more damage. So he, under my protest called for an ambulance.

The operator wanted to speak to me; I said to her 'I didn't want an ambulance as there are plenty more sick people than I out there'

She asked 'can I walk?'

'No' I cried in pain.

In the end I agreed to an ambulance.

Being on a remote tow-path Robie knew the ambulance people would struggle a little to find us so he ran along the path to the nearest road and called them again to give a better location, after about fifteen-twenty minutes they arrived with a stretcher trolley rattling over the rough stony muddy path.

Soon as I saw it I said to them quite indignantly 'I'm not getting on that thing, I'm not that bad'

In the end I agreed to travel on it, under one condition. This being that I must be covered with a sheet and they must play along with whatever I say or do, because from past knowledge wherever there is an ambulance there is always a crowd watching.

They agreed so we made our way to the waiting vehicle that was parked some distance back down the stony muddy path.

The ambulance was parked on the top of a small bridge which spanned the canal, there were a few people on the top of the bridge watching me being bumped along the path to the waiting vehicle, as soon as I saw them I started to say in a very loud voice, be careful of my baby, mind the big stones. They heard this from the bridge but what they didn't hear was the ambulance crew laughing'

I reminded them 'you promised, you must play along' which they did, marvellously.

'Now, now, there, there'

They were saying very loudly

'You and your baby will be just fine, just hold on, deep breaths'

'We'll be there soon' they chimed in synchronicity.

As we were drawing nearer to the people beside the ambulance I started to scream; 'it's coming! It's coming! Hurry, please hurry my baby is coming'

Well, all of the people around started to gossip amongst themselves.

'Oh she's a bit old for being pregnant isn't she' one said.

'She must be at least 60, the poor child. Fancy having a granny as a mother'

I was bundled into the back of the ambulance strapped in and we drove off laughing.

I was taken to Paddington hospital, London; they examined me, scanned me and took me off for an x-ray. It turned out that I had twisted my ankle very badly; I was black and blue from my waist to my little toe, and in lots of pain.

My other son Anthony called me on the phone to find out where I was as he had just returned from being away sailing for a month around France and Spain. When I told him he came in the car to collect us.

What with the commotion and pain of the day I had completely forgotten about the party booked for 6 in Chelsea until the next day. Robie wanted me to cancel the party because I was in so much pain, but I said to him '6 people have booked and they are leaving their work and they are looking forward to it' so I asked Robie to drive me there and carry in my case of cards and things, I hobbled in on two crutches, much to the surprise of my clients.

I had no idea how I was going to do this in this pain; I laid out my cards and got settled. The first person sat down and the pain literally vanished and left me instantly: talk about healing in action.

I started work all of the readings went well; the girl who organised the Chelsea party got a real warning that night about driving around Spain, she promised me she would not.

When I saw her a few months later she said I must tell you Collette, 'I wished I listen to you, I was stopped twice in Spain by the police whilst driving' What a silly girl.

After I finished the readings, the pain returned with vengeance. Spirit are wonderful, the power of their healing always surprises me, after this party I had four months of pain on crutches. But whenever I had a consultation to do, the pain would just disappear. It's the same even with a headache or if I'm feeling down.

Unbelievable!

* * *

Teddington Lock;

A mother never really forgets....

A woman who was about 65 years old had a reading, I did just her future; that's all she wanted.

After her consultation, she seemed not too happy at all, her future (3 months) looked okay so I couldn't work it out. But something was definitely wrong with this woman's peace of mind.

I said to her whilst I held her hand;

'This has not answered something you really wanted to know has it?'

She shook her head to say no.

I then said 'look, I'm sorry but for some reason I only read for three months' the poor woman started to cry, she said 'my mother had Alzheimer's disease and I'm terrified to get it'

I was still holding her hand at this time, and I said, 'if you get stressed about things you will not remember things and then because of your mothers illness you imagine you are getting it too, more stress more forgetting. Do you see the pattern?

I continued by saying 'so don't draw it to you'

Still the tears were there, streaming down her face.

I suddenly saw her mother, she was saying 'tell her she will not get it and I'm better now I'm here in spirit; and I will watch over her'

I shared this knowledge with her, she smiled whilst still crying.

I enquired to the woman, 'your mother decided to keep her hair long didn't she?'

'Yes' she said

'And she is tall and thin?'

'Yes'

'And she was put away as she was pretty crazy?'

'Yes' the lady replied

'And she died around 55 years due to tablets?

To this the lady just nodded.

What I would have done without her mother popping in at the right time, or be it a bit late; I don't really know.

I gave her a meditation cd and she left with her mind at peace, it always strikes me as funny that our parents don't leave us; I can't wait to haunt my kids, ha-ha –ha.

* * *

Somerset;
Never say goodbye.

A very quiet thinish girl wanted a reading, the link with her started at the first card, I kept seeing a man in a bed, so I just carried on with the next few cards but I always being drawn back to this older man laying there motionless in a bed. I'm in a hospital ward but I felt everybody was as sick as he was; they were all very seriously sick.

I don't like giving bad news but I will if spirit shows it to me a few times; as they know how I work.

The man looked more like a grandfather flat on his back. But I felt he was her father, I had to speak and now was the time.

I watched this young girls face very carefully (every muscle)

I asked 'do you know a man who is in a hospital bed, right now?'

'Yes' she said.

'Do you know this man is very, very sick?' I asked, I was now watching every muscle closely.

'Yes' she replied again.

I then asked spirit 'how far should I go?'

'All the way!' they replied.

I then said to the girl 'he is going to die. You know this don't you?'

With her eyes lowered, 'Yes' she said.

'This man is your father; he is with us because he must be

unconscious at this time. You are very close to each other and you have left his side to be here. And you will go back to him at the hospice as soon as you leave won't you?'

'Yes that's right' she said, fairly shocked.

'Well the reason he is here is to tell you and prove it through me today that you are close and to say that you both will be even closer when he is dead, in a few days time'

It was sad to have to say this to this young girl, and do you know what she said to me? She was pleased her dad would be out of pain, and that they would be close together.

Afterwards she shook my hand and with a choked smile and holding back her tears she left. I don't think I will forget the love between those two; it was lovely.

* * *

Elephant & Castle;
Mixing Spirits

The phone rang one day and the lady on the other end said, 'I own the Albert pub, it's at the Elephant and Castle. You did a reading for two of my barmaids at an event last weekend and I wondered if you could read for me, as they have recommended you?

I was a little taken back with her forthrightness, so I just said 'yes'.

'I can't get away from the pub though' she continued.

I replied 'that's okay; I will come to you, that's what I do. As I don't have people at my house; otherwise I have no home life'

I couldn't believe her name, I have never heard it before; Dawkus.

When I turned up a week later at the pub she took me upstairs, I hadn't even had the time to get my cards out and there by her side were three women. I ignored this for a while as spirit often queue up whilst I am preparing. During the consultation I was staring into the cards and I could see Dawkus running down the street chasing a piece of paper, it looked A4 size, and it's just keeps dancing down the street with the wind always just out of reach.

I told her this and she understood.

I said 'it looks like a driving licence you are chasing, Ahh, I see now, you and your husband are parting company' just as I said that the picture changed and she caught the piece of paper.

I asked her 'do remember the piece of paper?'

'Yes' she said

'Well I have just seen you catch it' I assured her

'Oh good' Dawkus said, 'it's the licence for this pub and I've applied for it to be in my name' 'well' I said, 'you will get it, don't worry'

I asked her 'when you are down stairs in the bar area I can see you moving lots of bottles around, do you often feel somebody touching your shoulder?'

'That's right' she said 'I do'

'Well I will tell you who it is, it's your grandmother and you feel other types of energies around you don't you?' '

Yes' she said.

'The other people here are your great aunts, it's funny they have come to you; they are telling me that you come from Cornwall, the whole family'

'Yes' she said 'we did'

'One of the other ladies is now taking me across the water on a map and it's stopping at Lyon in France. Do you know why?

Dawkus just shook her head, no

I said 'Dawkus, if you ever get a chance could you research this please?' 'Well' she said 'I have heard my grandmother mention that they came from France, 100's of years ago'

We progressed onto Dawkus' future which looked good.

A couple of years later I went back to the pub with a friend, I couldn't see Dawkus anywhere, so I enquired to the barmaid after her.

'No she said she sold and left last year. I know who you are though; I am the barmaid you read for a few years ago and I've still got your card.

Will you please come for an evening here so that we can, perhaps mix spirits together'

I didn't get the joke at first, so she explained it to me.

Ha-ha.

* * *

Greenford;
Green Condom

As I was looking into this young lady's present cards, an old lady appeared. She had short curly grey hair, a long woollen coat, a rather large handbag and a hat. I know that this describes millions of grandparents.

So I asked the old lady 'please find something this young girl can recognise, something that I can give to her'

She went off for a few minutes and then came back, she said 'tell her I was her next door neighbour' so I described her to the young girl, her face looked like 'I don't really believe you'

I mentally said to the old lady 'it's got to be a lot more than this you must return with something more hard hitting, something more concrete'

So back to the cards we went. In the cards I could see her mother was having a lot of problems with her health, I put this to her and she just replied 'yes, will she be okay?

My guide gave me a picture of bare feet ascending rocky hills with large boulders strewn across the pathway. Yet although the heels of the feet were cut and bleeding they were still climbing, bearing through the pain; to get to the end.

I said to the girl 'your mum will have a few tough times, very painful & difficult times, your mum will make it. So don't worry.

Hard hitting!! I don't believe what I am looking at! I said to the young girl, this old lady is back she says 'she knows about the green condom'

Well I laughed at the girl's embarrassment, I just couldn't help it.

I find that spirit can have such a sense of humour, and yet be so full of light, love and healing (holy in other words) I do like their humour though.

She did not know where to put her face, to make her feel better I said

'I don't think I would like a green one'

We both laughed. I said 'we won't delve further into that one. This old lady is showing me a kitchen; it's narrow and brilliant yellow, do you know it?'

'Yes' she said very shocked. 'it's mine!'

'Well this lady does visit and to prove more she is the one who moves the pots that are hanging on the wall. She tells me that when she was here on earth she did this in your kitchen'

Oh gosh' she replied 'I do know who she is; she lived next door to us for years. I had forgotten'

'She never forgot you, did she?' I remarked she says that it is her that has been looking after you and your mum; for years.

* * *

Thames Riverside;
You've gotta have faith...

A very nice black security guard showed us to our pitch; I said to my son's 'you know what? She's a really lovely person'

Just as we got setup for the day she came for a reading, she sat down and took her security jacket off so that she would be lost in the crowds of thousands.

During her consultation a nice black man appeared his hair was so grey, it's very difficult to put an age on a black man going by their hair as they are very lucky and don't age till very late. So I don't really know if this granddad or dad I'm looking at. He just stood there for a while as I was doing her cards for the present.

Just before I went onto her future cards, I was the transported to her bathroom, I was watching her looking in the bathroom mirror and she could see her father in the mirror.

I said to her, 'you have never told anybody that you see your father in the bathroom mirror have you?

In floods of tears she said to me 'so it's real then, I really do see my dad? 'Yes' I replied, 'he's just standing there beside you'

I got on with her future. And we parted.

Next thing the rest of the security staff were trying to get a reading, but they couldn't get the time of work to see me that day and we were booked up anyway; as we often are, very quickly.

The next day when we pulled onto the site the young man security person on the gate said 'Name?'

I replied 'Collette Star'

'So, you're Collette Star are you?' he said. Straight away I became like an eight years old child again, always in trouble, never conform and always an individual.

'Oh what have I done wrong' I enquired gingerly.

He said, 'you have been causing arguments since 7am'

'I said how? I was still in bed'

He replied 'well you read for a few people yesterday and the rest of the security team wants a reading with you. All of them are trying to fit their breaks around you'

I did feel honoured by these security people; I just hoped that I did their faith justice.

* * *

Kew Fayre;
The Wonderful Love

Kerry who runs Kew Fayre wanted a reading. Oh how I hate being put on the spot like this.

We had completed her past cards, we had also moved onto the present; during which an old man popped in, I described to her how he used to collect her when she was about 6 year old. They would hold hands and go up a lane past some council red brick looking houses to his allotment, where they spent many happy times together.

He says 'he has been watching you and the children and he will help you with your future, he tells me that you miss him so much, but there is no need as he is with you quite a lot, he knows the wonderful love you have for him. He says that he will stay here whilst I do your future reading'

Well, I couldn't be that bad as she still talks to me, and I am the only clairvoyant allowed to have a pitch at this annual event.

* * *

Putney;
Do you mind!........ Ma'am....

A lady rang for a private reading at her home; she took my card from an event and decided to ring me. She had a very posh accent, her name was Pamela. So I went with an open mind as I always do, I think it was one of the weirdest experiences I have had.

She lived in a great big house, almost mansion like; I was led down to the basement which opened out into an enormous kitchen. She looked at me quite sternly and sort of proclaimed, 'we can go into the garden if you would like'

'Oh yes' I quickly and curtly replied 'I would much prefer that'

I always have my tape recorder with me; I put it on the table and laid out the cards. Tea soon arrived so we started. But every time I tried to pick up from spirit what they were trying to tell me, she kept telling me to; 'turn the tape on' which I did, and then 'turn it off' and so on.

I thought, I just can't work like this. Does she not understand what a fine line speaking to spirit is? It' hard enough without her incessant interruptions 'Turn it on, turn it off'

I said excuse me, 'I know what I am doing, I am trying to talk to somebody for you and you just keep interfering, please let me do my work'

She shut up for a minute; I could see a stick with a silver knob, which was very significant for this man. He had clothing like 16th century Dickens time with white or cream clinging trousers, but it was his attitude he came in with, 'you should not be here! Sat in her presence' you should be serving her, how dare you sit there'

He then chimed up again 'I say, how dare you wench'

Well, I was shocked, even more shocked when she carried on about the blessed tape again. 'Turn it on, turn it off'

So I turned it on and told her about the man. I then went back to the man asking for more, and just as the silver tipped stick came back again, Pamela piped up again 'turn on and turn it off'

As you can imagine, rage was building inside (I am only human after all)

I lost it, and in a calm fashion but very firm I said,

'I know I'm in your home and you are my client, but firstly I don't need your custom, secondly you are not my boss; my 'head office' is my only law I obey (spirit) so would you like me to leave. Or are you going to behave yourself and leave the sitting to me?'

Well bless her she hung her head with the rest of her future cards.

The man from the gentry who thought I should be 'below stairs' (servant) just stood there with his nose in the air quite indignantly. Pamela asked me when I finally got the whole description of the man, 'to describe his hair'

I said 'I don't know, it is being hidden somehow from me'

When we finished she took me upstairs to a big room full of beautiful antiques. There he was, stood before me in a huge 4ft portrait painting; of the very man that I had been describing downstairs, complete with the silver knob stick and clingy trousers.

I said to her 'now I know why they hid the hair from me, I would have thought it would have come from my own mind and I may have rejected him completely'

There he was in a Perry wig, before me in the portrait. 'A real

17th century toff' No wonder why he thought I should be 'below stairs' (servant) and not sat in his great, great, great etc granddaughters presence.

I have been back a few times to read from Pamela, and she has always been a good lady about the tape. We have become friends and go out together, to dinner parties and the like. I bet he doesn't like that.

The snob!

* * *

Brockwell Park;
I don't look when they have sex!

A woman with a push chair, 2 kids and a husband arrived. He took the children away so that she could be with me; alone.

What a nice little family I thought.

As I picked the cards up, the clairvoyance started. I was in her bedroom, well, I thought I was her bedroom, but just to be on the safe side I asked her 'don't you keep your bedroom tidy?' she looked a bit puzzled at me, 'Yes' she replied inquisitively

I then said 'the net curtains move in your room as if there is a slight wind pushing them don't they?

'Yes, I have noticed that' she replied.

'And do you feel sometimes that when you are in your bed you feel that somebody has sat or is sitting on the end of your bed?'

She looked startled, 'yes that's right'

'I'm being told that it's your dad' I laughingly remarked.

'Oh' she simply replied.

With all sorts of thoughts rushing through her mind!

She was starting to get upset. But because of this, her dad said 'tell her I don't look when they have sex! I always look the other way' and with that he laughed. I passed this on; she laughed, but cried at the same time.

I don't know what people must think when they walk past and see me and the sitter laughing, or crying?

After she had her future section of the consultation done she left with her tape. After about eight more clients, she was back but this time with her husband and the rest of her family in tow; so that they could have a reading.

* * *

Somerset;
Oh Susan; your Mum knows now......

There was another stall holder called Susan, she is a nice little girl a bit scatty though, but so am I. She looked like some young hippy girl, so you can imagine it surprised me when I found out later she was a teacher.

Throughout the weekend she kept saying to Anthony 'I must have a reading with your mum, I must have a reading before I go' in between selling her clothes and jewellery.

A lady sat down, she had short grey hair. I got to work.

I immediately felt that I was at the seaside, the Isle of Wight in fact. I told her that I could see in her cards that she was very worried about her mother's cancer of the womb.

'How do you know that?' she said

I replied 'I don't know how it just happens. I am better with some people than others, but how I know she lives at the seaside is down to these Runes that I keep on my table. I treat them like pebbles, and when somebody lives by the sea, spirit makes me pick them up and I grind them in my hand, that's how I know'

I said to the lady 'I will tell a very funny tale about a time when I was in Worthing, Sussex, along the windy sea front.

A very pompous lady was staring at the Runes on my table from a distance, and quite rudely she just walked up during a consultation with another person and in a very condescending posh voice she said 'what is the significance of placing the Runes onto each card?'

Oh she was so pompous! So I said in my worst cockney accent I could muster

'It stops the cards from blowin away, din it'

Then she walked off. Oh dear. It was much funnier being there though.

The lady before me found this very funny which cheered her up about her mum; we carried on with her reading.

I said to her 'don't worry, your mum will be okay, it's just a scare; she hasn't got it'

We moved on a bit, I then said 'now, are you a grandmother aren't you? 'No' she replied 'Categorically No!'

'Well' I said 'there is most definitely a baby on its way, and you will be a grandmother soon. I can see this baby'

'There better not be' she retorted. 'My daughter is not in the position to have a child'

'They are not always planned you know, not by us anyway' I cautiously replied.

She was not a happy lady so when I finished her future she took her tape and left.

A few more people came and went and then a very good looking grey headed man came from the crowded marquee and sat down.

I said to him, 'I am being shown a shower, in an office; it's your office, how weird. When you go in this shower you can hear spirit talk to you can't you?' he looked at me in shock.

'Ahh, Ahh' I said as I wagged my finger at him.

'They are telling me all of your secrets aren't they? And there is trouble with your business, isn't there?

He just sat there dumb founded with what to say.

I continued 'they are saying don't get het up and you will think clearly, you will have some news in the family and spirit want you to keep cool when all around you are not. When all are screaming and shouting, you will need to have a family get together, to discuss a problem. And I want you to be strong, nobody is going to die or have a horrible accident, I know that much so please don't think that way'

You have a good three months future, take your tape; it's all on there. He left slightly puzzled.

Half an hour before the marquee shut, Susan who had the stall near my son and I made it to me.

The first thing I saw was a man; he was like a father figure. He was very disillusioned in her and they just kept on quarrelling, I asked her this and she just put her head down and said 'Yes' This is just how she is.

Then I could see that she was pregnant and there was going to be a lot of family rows, I also could see she was in lots of pain with the love that had let her down. I told her this, with that she started to cry and she said 'I thought I had got over him'

'No' I said 'emotion has no time.

Take for example; if I made you recall something very emotional, good or bad. If you recall it properly all of the anger will still be there, 10, 20 or even 30 years on. Only the rough edges will be removed. So time is not a great healer; but simply a rounder of edges'

'Now dry your eyes and let's look at your future'

'Susan, you have not told them you're pregnant have you? It's all here in the cards'

'No' she said.

'Your parents will understand I'm sure' I said trying to comfort her.

'No they won't! You should know, you've just read for them today'

'What!' I gasped.

'They are here' she said pointing down the marquee, 'over there, see the short lady with the grey hair; that's my mum'

'Oh no, Susan. She knows now'

'How, how does she know?' she enquired panic-stricken.

I replied hesitantly and tongue in cheek 'I told her in her reading that she's going to be a grandmother, and she was not pleased at all; and now I know why'

I then asked her 'point out your dad to me please'

'He's right down the bottom, the tall man with grey hair'

She said looking at me very worriedly.

'Oh Susan, he knows about a family upsetment' I gravely told her.

She just laughed, it was a nervous laugh.

I did tell her that I could see her and her dad becoming friends again. She was so pleased she started crying again, she is so scatty, so disorganised mentally. But I do like her very much.

She's one of those people in life that will mess everything up if it's not messed up already. She is a child herself in a grown up world and she's lovely.

* * *

Basingstoke;
Sunshine Face

A young lady that I had read for the previous year brought an old man to me.

116

She said 'this is the man that you told me last year was going to be very ill, and you said don't worry he will not die, he will pull through' 'Well here he is, fit and well. You were right he was extremely ill and I thought you were wrong about him dying'

She continued without hesitation, 'is it possible we could both get a reading with you?'

I call her 'sunshine face' she is blonde, of a very happy disposition with freckles and she is about 28 years old.

She has had a rough time getting off drugs but she has done it. She is a very nice person.

We couldn't fit them both in, as I had only one space left. Typically she gave hers up for him.

What a lovely man he was, a lady popped in, she had long dark hair. She seemed Spanish/Italian she said 'ask him about the allotments' I told him this and he laughed and enquired 'which one? I have twelve!'

'My god, no wonder she said 'ask you about the allotments' what a lot of work' I replied shocked. 'Ahh wait a minute, it's the one with the new shed, and in the left hand corner of the new shed you hear a woman talking to you, don't' you?'

'Yes' he said very proudly with his eyes widening.

I said 'It's your wife; she has long dark hair and a bit foreign looking, isn't she?'

'Yes that's right, lovely woman, dammed fine she was' he replied very proudly again.

I continued 'She tells me you miss her a lot, you hear her and talk to her'

He nodded, but with his lips now quite tight; and doing fairly well not to burst.

'Could you please stand up' I asked.

Which he did; and with that I put my arms around him and we cuddled each other in front of everybody.

With his wife's permission, of course.

'This is what you miss' I said.

'Ahh yes' he said 'I do'

I told him, 'if I were 15 or 20 years older I would have you for myself'

He was so lovely.

'I would not refuse you' he said.

We sat down and got on with his future.

'You will see me again next year' he said smiling as he left. 'Goodbye'

* * *

Cambridge;
A Clean Habit.

My son Robie said 'Mum, this lady here has been waiting for you. She said she wants some healing; not from me. She insists that it is from you'

'Ok, Robie' I said 'show her a seat; after this reading I will see to her'

I came around the side of the van to see her sat there, she was wearing a white jumper with a great big bump; she was very pregnant.

I never talk to people if I can help it, as I feel it is not my place. I hand everything over to my guides as they know what is needed, not I.

I said to her 'just shut your eyes, say nothing please and enjoy it'

She did, and she was completely gone.

This does seem to happen to people, I don't touch them; they just go unconscious.

It's like I'm a telephone operator just connecting two people together 'long-distance' the person and the spirit.

Whilst they are out cold I leave my guides and their guides working together. I just walk off and do something else. It can take them along time to come around, but because of her condition I said to Robie, 'I am going to get a tea. Watch over her, do not let her go. I really do need to talk to her! Robie it is imperative'

He knows I would not carry on like this if I didn't think that it was important. I returned just as she was coming round in her chair. Robie got her a cup of tea, and I sat with her. I tried to explain what happens.

'Your baby, who happens to have been a monk last time has said you are afraid and it is affecting the baby, and it will make the baby ill. What's the matter? Have you not had a baby before?'

'Oh it's not that' she replied 'I've been told that when the baby is born, during the birth, my baby could develop some fatal disease'

I said 'his guide is here with him' and it's his guide that has passed on this information. Oh yes it is a boy by the way.

'Oh' she said 'I didn't know'

I carried on 'Well he's feeling all this fear in you, and it's not doing him any good'

'So please stop the fear, it will be okay. I've been told to mention 'Grey friars' to you. Apparently your baby and his guide was in the Grey Friars order.

I don't know anything about the grey ones; you could look it up, this may help to take your entire mind away from this.

He will be fine, just stop the fear. Please'

When she felt straight again she got up and left.

I didn't forget her, I often wondered about her.

The following year we returned to Cambridge. I know the field is big, but I was hoping to see her. Alas she did not turn up....

The following year, I was asked to do some healing on a man, out cold he went, afterwards I gave him a cup of tea whilst his wife had a reading, the child in the pushchair was oddly very quiet. Thank god!

I do like children, but not when I'm working.

At the end of her reading she looked at me and said 'you don't remember me do you?'

I said 'I am sorry, I really do see hundreds of people, and I can't recognise everybody'

'Well' she said, 'this is the baby you said would be fine, here he is and very fit'

I could not tell you how delighted I was.

Even now I have big lump in my throat just thinking about it.

I said to her, 'I have been worried about you. I never did forget you, only your face'

She smiled and said 'I tried to find you last year'

I thanked her and said 'I was hoping to see you also, but when I didn't; I feared the worst'

'No' she said, 'his birth was great, you were so right, and I kept listening to your meditation cd. Your cd is great'

'But get this!' she gushed 'the school he goes to is called 'Grey Friars'

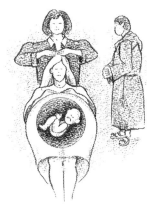

She then said 'It sends a shiver down my spine when I think of the conversations you must have with the spirit world'

With that her husband was ready to leave; and I, as usual had more booked readings. So we said goodbye for another year. Just as they were leaving the little boy in the pushchair gave me a lovely big smile as if he knew.

* * *

Cambridge;
Resistance Healing

When I dislocated my shoulder whilst doing silly things in France, I went to see my friend Antonio for some healing as he is exceptional.

Whilst I was there he went out to his big garden with some bread for the birds. Upon his return he was carrying a gun, a skinny looking long rifle over his shoulder. He had a black beret cocking slightly to one side on his head.

I thought I was seeing things for a moment, but he wasn't walking up the garden as described earlier. He looked just the same as he does today, but I could see him on top of a hill and I could see rabbits running around and I seemed to know that this person shoots them. I felt I was on a border of countries. And I was waiting for something.

As I looked closer; he was older than Antonio and smoking which Antonio doesn't.

This man was in the resistance, the Spanish one.

I asked Antonio about the gun and I told him what I was seeing.

He said 'Yes my father used to shoot rabbits up in the hills. I still have the gun locked up in Spain'

Antonio also said 'I was told that my father did help out during World War 2 but I never did know much about it, as it was all top secret'

So we progressed with the healing of the shoulder.

* * *

London;
Love thy Neighbour......

When I first moved into my current residence which is an apartment overlooking the river Thames, I often would look out at night upon the passing boats and people wandering along the riverside walk.

One night whilst looking from the window I noticed an old lady from next door also looking out over the river. I waved to her and she was delighted that somebody was waving to her.

A few days later we met in the communal entrance, we introduced ourselves and shook hands; she left and I went inside. I then said to my two sons 'I've just met the old lady from next door, what a lovely soul'.

We would meet at the window most nights; it became a sort of ritual before we both went to bed.

In the summer we started to chat with the windows open, Floss told me that she was an 87 year old widow, with no social life and her kids didn't put much time or effort in either, so consequently she was very depressed and miserable.

She told me one day 'I'm so happy you came here to live Collette; life was not worth living, I just existed'.

Our friendship soon progressed to a cup of tea.

She became very fond of my sons Anthony & Robie, and even though she was terrified by dogs, after a while she was able to give 'Honey' our golden retriever a biscuit, whilst shaking with terror.

Over the next few years our friendship grew and grew, and she became my dearest friend, we would go to the theatre together, ice shows and family dinners; in short she became my mum. Our relationship was so strong that she could tell me off if she thought I was wrong, I didn't mind though as sometimes I was wrong and when I was, I accepted it.

Although Floss was a staunch Roman Catholic, she became very interested about Spiritualism and other people's views once she found out about the recently finished 'Pure & Simple' tarot/divination pack and that I was a medium.

She was very psychic herself but was unaware of her talents. With this in mind I asked her to look at the original drawings and tell me as I held each one up what she felt they portrayed to her. She did extremely well; out of the 44 drawings there were only 2 she did not get absolutely correct.

After I told her of her success and what they were, she told me that she felt very sinful, because in her religion she should not be doing this.

Floss said that she will have to go on the bus to the Cathedral in

Victoria in order to pray for forgiveness.

Well I did laugh at Floss, 'it's all the same thing' I said to her.

We would talk for hours and hours on the subject, our friendship became so strong that she would cry and get very depressed if I went on holiday or just away for a couple of days.

A few years and many happy hours between us went by.

One day I took Floss for an x-ray to St Thomas' Hospital as she had a lot of pain in her arm. Her family should have been doing this sort of thing but they were continuously lacking in their duties.

The pain never appeared to leave her, the hospital said that she had not broken any bones, so she just had to put up with it and there's nothing wrong.

The pain went on for months, eventually the pain was so bad the hospital admitted her to a ward, they found out after numerous tests that she unfortunately had bone cancer. I was away on one of my trips at the time so I wasn't around to help her.

When I returned I learnt of what had happened and I would visit her every couple of days. But the pain for her was getting worst by the day.

The hospital forced her out into a residential nursing home, although her children had mountains of space, nobody offered, I did miss her at the window and her visiting me, but we could at least have our spiritual/religious conversations at her bedside.

One day she seemed to know that she wasn't coming home again, she held my hand and said, 'I love you Collette'

'I also love you Floss, but you know that don't you?' I replied

'Yes I do' she said whilst nodding fraily.

She continued 'Collette, I really hope you are here when I go' (die)

I looked at her and replied 'Floss, there is no need to be afraid, you will see your husband Ernie, and there will be no fear, you will go with him into the light'.

She squeezed my hand and said 'thank you'.

The next day she took a very bad turn for the worst, and within two days she was gone. I had lost my good friend, Floss.

Three days later whilst sitting in my dressing gown in the lounge drinking my morning coffee, in walked Floss. I never expected this, well, not so early anyway. She walked across the floor and sat in a seat that she had never sat in before, I said 'Floss, it's lovely to see you but why are you sat in that chair? You're normally sat in that one' as I pointed to a dining room chair.

She replied simply 'I can see you better from here'.

I just laughed & I said 'I am sorry I was not there'.

'Oh that's ok Collette, you were right about death; there's really nothing to fear, and its lovely' she replied.

With that she disappeared, and I just mentally thought,

'Well Floss, you've made the connection, so I'll be seeing you soon'.

She pops back now and then, but I know it may get less and less as the years progress, or maybe not, we'll just have to see.

The front of the 'Pure & Simple' tarot/divination box depicts Floss' favourite card, she chose this as her favourite when she read them previously, she never knew its name; it's called peace.

When Floss died she left me her rosary beads and her large onyx cross, but more importantly; her love.

* * *

London;

Anthony, my dad and my uncle.

My son Anthony was talking to me in the front room one day whilst accompanied by my dad at his side. No surprise there as this is often the case, the situation I find the funniest is when my dad, Anthony and my uncle are all sat on the settee together like a right little family.

There have been many times when we are all sat listening to Anthony just chatting away and the only one unaware of what is happening is Anthony; as he thinks he's only talking to me and not to my dad and uncle as well who have just popped in for a visit.

Over the years he has learnt that if my eyes move slightly to his side and I smile, he then knows that we have a couple of spirit visitors.

On this particular occasion though, when Anthony got up and left the room to make a cup of tea, I noticed that my dad was walking inches from his back, he even stood behind him at the sink and then at the kettle.

My dad was wearing his vest which depicts the summer for me; it's currently April.

As my dad and I looked at each other he said to me 'I am going to stick close to the boy, all this summer, as he's going to need a lot of strength'

I then asked my dad telepathically 'why?'

He just tapped his nose as he always did when I was young and said 'mind your own business, leave it to me and don't worry'

(Well, now I am worried)

I called out to Anthony 'are you driving tomorrow?'

(Anthony drives the elderly and special needs children for the local council)

'No mum, I've got to do management stuff in the office; why?' he replied.

'Well' I replied 'my dad is stuck to you like glue out there, and he says that he's going to look after you, and that you will need strength this summer'

Anthony didn't say a word but probably thought; 'mad mothers at it again'

Next day Anthony called me and said 'you know I was to be in the office today'

I said coldly and inquisitively whilst holding my breath 'Yes'

He then went on to say 'Well mum, they put me out on the road due to lack of staff and a big red London Double Decker bus came right through the back of the bus I was driving and smashed it to bits! It came through right behind where I was sitting! But what's really odd is that just before the crash I was due to pick up a single passenger who is an elderly lady and she always sits right where the bus came crashing through, regardless of other occupants on the bus.

Lucky for her and very unusually she decided to walk home 5 mins before I arrived to collect her, and 7 mins before the crash. The big red London bus would have killed her stone dead as the windows and seats all down one side were all pushed in and towards the other side of the bus. How the bus missed me I don't know! Your dad was right'

I said 'Anthony, dad told me that it will be all the summer he will stick by you, so it's not over yet'

About four weeks later I was on a train to visit a friend suddenly my dad pops in and there he was sat opposite me in the carriage, he looked at me and remarked with urgency 'ring the boy and tell him, somebody is going to put pressure on him. Tell him to take no notice and don't listen. The boy must be very careful, tell him now' he then disappeared as quickly as he arrived.

When I got off the train I called Anthony and asked 'are you ok?'

'Yes mum, why?' he replied

I informed him that 'My dad has just popped in and said you are to be careful as somebody will put pressure on you to do something, and he says that you should take no notice'

My friend then arrived in her car; I said to Anthony 'well I have told you what he said and I've got to go now, I'll see you later'

That night Anthony returned home and he walked into my office, and said 'your dad was right again'

'Why what's happened?' I replied

He said 'I went skating on one of the 'London skates' (www.londonskaters.com/video-london-skate.htm & www.lfns.co.uk) and I was hit by a bike so I had to take a controlled fall'

There he stood with his trousers ripped to shreds and his knee pads and wrist guards looked more like they had been attacked by an industrial grinder, luckily no injuries though.

Anthony continued 'I only went because a chap at work wanted to go skating as he bought some skates a while ago and hadn't been out on them yet'

I thought about it for a minute and replied 'Ah yes, but do you remember what my dad said about somebody putting a big pressure on you?'

God bless my dad, may he look after us; always.

Acknowledgements

I would like to thank my son Anthony for his never-ending patience, his vast encouragement and understanding and without his computer and editing skills each story would not have come to life.

To John Gibbins for the amazing illustrations throughout this book, to his wife Claudette for the great lunches and to his son Christian; for all his help.

Finally to Timothy, who is my Clairvoyance guide; without him none of this would *ever* have taken place.

BOOKS

O is a symbol of the world, of oneness and unity. In different cultures it also means the "eye", symbolizing knowledge and insight. We aim to publish books that are accessible, constructive and that challenge accepted opinion, both that of academia and the "moral majority".

Our books are available in all good English language bookstores worldwide. If you don't see the book on the shelves ask the bookstore to order it for you, quoting the ISBN number and title. Alternatively you can order online (all major online retail sites carry our titles) or contact the distributor in the relevant country, listed on the copyright page.

See our website www.o-books.net for a full list of over 400 titles, growing by 100 a year.

And tune in to myspiritradio.com for our book review radio show, hosted by June-Elleni Laine, where you can listen to the authors discussing their books.

MySpiritRadio

SOME RECENT O BOOKS

Spirit Release
Sue Allen

This book is the most comprehensive I have seen on the subject of spirit release. For some, this subject matter could be seen as terrifying, it is the stuff of horror films. Sue has a down to earth common sense approach that leaves you without fear and no doubt that what she is saying is accurate. This book is a must for anyone working and dealing with people. **Becky Walsh**, presenter of The Psychic Show on LBC
1846940338 256pp **£11.99 $24.95**

An Exchange of Love
Madeleine Walker

A lovely book with a gentle and profound message about how closely our animal companions are linked to our triumphs and traumas, and an astonishing insight into how willing they are to be a surrogate for our stress symptoms and how instrumental they can be in our healing. Madeleine Walker is one of the best animal intuitives in the world.
Kindred Spirit
978-1-84694-139-9 186pp **£9.99 $19.95**

Palmistry: From Apprentice to Pro in 24 Hours
The Easiest Palmistry Course Ever Written
Johnny Fincham

Straightforward and engaging, Johnny Fincham delivers exactly what is promised. A non-nonsense, common sense palmistry course which can be completed in twenty four one hour sessions. If you are interested in palmistry, this is definitely for you. Be prepared to embrace the new and leave mystification behind. The easiest to follow, scientifically based, training course on palmistry you can find today. **Light**
9781846940477 240pp **£9.99 $16.95**